Francis "TWO GUN" Crowley's
KILLINGS in
New York City & Long Island

Francis "TWO GUN" Crowley's
KILLINGS in
New York City & Long Island

Jerry Aylward

THE
History
PRESS

Published by The History Press
Charleston, SC
www.historypress.com

First published 2020

Manufactured in the United States

ISBN 9781467144353

Library of Congress Control Number: 2020934366

Notice: The information in this book is true and complete to the best of our knowledge. It is offered without guarantee on the part of the author or The History Press. The author and The History Press disclaim all liability in connection with the use of this book.

Dedicated to the memory of Patrolman Fred S. Hirsch Jr. and all the police officers who have made the ultimate sacrifice. May God provide wisdom, strength and safety to all those who continue to protect and serve the citizens of our great country.

Contents

Acknowledgements

To reassemble the fractured chain of violent events that occurred almost ninety years ago required the assistance, contributions and understanding of countless people, many not affiliated with the law enforcement community, and most unfamiliar with the story or the characters of those events, but all with a deep respect and appreciation for those in law enforcement who made the ultimate sacrifice. Some I met for the first time, a few others I have known for over thirty years, making it difficult to know who to thank first. I must apologize in advance if I have missed or overlooked anyone—please know that it wasn't intentional.

I'll begin with the valued assistance provided by Betsy Paradis, history and collections librarian at the Bangor, Maine public library, who was most helpful in digging through years of archived *Bangor Daily News* reports.

I'd also like to express my sincere gratitude to Emergency Services Unit police officer Nick Brilis (Ret.) of the Yonkers Police Department and the Yonkers Police Department's Historical Society for sharing its valued case knowledge, documents and photos of the 1931 Virginia Brannen murder investigation. It was also an honor to meet and work with such an insightful and dedicated police officer as Nick, with almost thirty years of committed service to the people of Yonkers and a lifelong resident of Yonkers. Nick's selfless devotion in preserving Yonkers police history—as well as his warm and welcoming professional courtesy—ranks him top honors among police history preservationists in the country.

I must also add another person to that list of knowledgeable, perceptive and dedicated police professionals, New York City Police Department's Lieutenant Michael Ryan (Ret.) from the office of the First Deputy Commissioner of Police, who was also NYPD's genealogist. Mike's contribution to this project was not only immensely valued but the speed and accuracy of his essential details also provided welcomed and rewarding relief to my research.

I would also like to thank Detective Sergeant Benjamin Gosun IV of the Support Services Bureau (SSB) Investigative Unit, for his valued knowledge, contribution and unending professional courtesy throughout this project.

I've been extremely fortunate during my research for this project to come into contact with the dedicated men and women of the New York State Department of Corrections. I have to express my sincere thanks to New York State Department of Corrections and Community Supervision commissioner Anthony J. Annucci for his approval and authorization to view the Crowley and Duringer records at the Sing Sing prison facility in Ossining, New York. Also, a very special thanks to three extraordinary men from that facility. They are Sing Sing Prison Superintendent Michael Capra, Lieutenant John Gilman and Sing Sing historian senior correction officer Arthur "Art" Wolpinsky. They offered me a virtual tour of their facility that very few people have ever taken (and lived to talk about), including a trip back through time to the 1931 death chamber. Plus, their assistance allowed me to view rare historic documents that verified and formulated some of the events in this book. I am also forever indebted to them for sharing their outstanding knowledge, extending their endless professional courtesy and their dedication to the preservation of the past. To quote Lieutenant John Gilman: "This story was our fate!"

Appreciation is also gratefully extended to the Nassau County Police Department in recognition for archived documents used in writing in this book.

Grateful appreciation to the Nassau County Police Museum, specifically Officer Steve Zacchia for providing the NCPD archived departmental police images. Steve was always a willing contributor who shared a special interest in this project.

In my endless search for archived and loss court records, I must thank Debbie Perez at the Nassau County Court Clerk's Office for her aid and patience in understanding my quest for historical case information on an eighty-nine-year-old murder case.

I would also like to thank Chief of Police Joe Burton (Ret.) of the Ossining New York Police Department, currently assisting the Ossining Historical Society in providing pertinent historical documentation relative to this project.

A special thank-you to Iris Levin of the Nassau County Museum's Photograph file unit, who provided some of the rare images in this project and was always quick to respond to my requests, though I'm sure she was busy with many other projects.

Particular thanks to Dr. Ellen H. Belcher, special collections librarian for the Lewis E. Lawes Papers, Lloyd Sealy Library, at John Jay College of Criminal Justice in New York City for her invaluable insight and contribution in providing me the opportunity to view the Lewis E. Lawes collection and images.

I must also thank the many research assistants at the National Archives and Records Administration and the Library of Congress in Washington, D.C., for their knowledge and guidance in assisting me with the collection of documentation in the genealogy research of this project.

My further thanks and respectful admiration to acquisitions editor J. Banks Smither and all in The History Press family for making it possible to tell the story of the heroic police officers and the other victims of a violent gangster's crime spree as he crisscrossed the many police boundary lines in New York on his murderous quest for glory.

Finally, I'd like to thank my dear friend and companion Anita Chen for her continued support, insight and helpful suggestions in dealing with the many different personalities and research avenues needed to maneuver this project to completion. A proud highball to my son, NYPD Special Operations sergeant Joe Aylward (Ret.), for his dedication and commitment in protecting the people of New York City. Thanks to Katie and Po Dawg as well.

Introduction

I first heard the name Fred S. Hirsch Jr. when I was in the Nassau County Police Academy, though I can't remember exactly the specific instructional course or the instructor. Still, I do remember the year the instructor said Fred S. Hirsch Jr. was murdered, 1931. But most of all, I remembered that he was the first Nassau County patrolman murdered in the line of duty. (He wasn't the first patrolman killed in the line of duty; that mournful destination would go to Patrolman John A. Hahn, who was killed in an accident while operating a departmental motorcycle on September 24, 1925, less than six months from the inception of the Nassau County Police Department.) What also stuck in my mine at the time was that Patrolman Fred S. Hirsch Jr. was ruthlessly gunned down by a guy named "Two Gun" Crowley. Not just someone named Crowley, or some criminal named Crowley, or even a New York City gangster named Francis Crowley. No, he was killed by a guy named Two Gun Crowley.

I distinctly recall thinking at the time that a moniker like "Two Gun" given to a guy who likes to shoot cops could actually elevate that killer's criminal status to a greater notoriety, like a celebrity status among other cop killers, or at least in his own mind. I know if you had asked anyone in my academy class the day following that lecture what Hirsch's first name was, few, if any would remember, but I'm absolutely sure, most, if not all, would remember the killer was a guy named "Two Gun" something or another. So who gave Crowley that name, I wondered? Was it the police, the media or his criminal cohorts? It was obvious to most of us that criminals, even gangsters, didn't carry two guns or even need two guns. The academy instructor couldn't provide the answer either.

Many years later, when I was assigned to the detective squad in the First Precinct in Baldwin, New York (Patrolman Fred Hirsch's precinct—they were called patrolman then, now they're called police officers), I was told by a veteran street cop the fragmented version of the early morning hours of May 6, 1931. He even took me to the approximate spot where Patrolman Fred Hirsch was gunned down and died, shot by "Two Gun" Crowley. I say approximate because there are no markers, plaques or anything to indicate that the thirty-one-year-old police officer, husband and father of four died a sudden and violent death on a dirt lane in a remote wooden area of North Merrick, New York, while the rest of the world slept peacefully. Ironically, it was also the same dirt lane that was used exclusively by local lovers.

Hirsch was ambushed by a vicious, two gun–toting psychopathic gangster out of control on a wild three-month murderous crime spree through Long Island, New York City and Yonkers, New York, to feed an enlarged narcissistic ego. Actually, his spree of murder, robbery and assault lasted exactly seventy-five days. In that short time, however, Two Gun Crowley left an evil wake of one dead Nassau County patrolman, one brutally murdered twenty-three-year-old taxi dance hall dancer, one New York City detective shot and fighting for his life, one wealthy real estate developer shot five times as Crowley invaded his home during a robbery attempt and two others in yet another violent incident who suffered serious gunshot wounds by Two Gun Crowley, in his need for an equalizer. Plus, there were countless other victims known and unknown who had been forced to face down the terrorizing barrels of this gangster's guns.

At 12:48 a.m. on May 6, 1931, Francis "Two Gun" Crowley became the subject of one of the largest and most comprehensive police manhunts in the history of the New York metropolitan area. Over eighteen thousand police officers actively searched for the violent little gangster. At the time, it was the most extensive manhunt ever generated by New York–area police. The massive dragnet stretched from the eastern tip of Long Island to include all of New York City and up into Westchester County, including bordering states. Shoot on sight orders were given to all law enforcement officers, as the police were determined to end Crowley's violent reign of terror against law enforcement and the citizens of New York.

Some people would say that anytime one human being takes the life of another that it should always be considered murder, and as such, the killing of a human being would be a criminal act, regardless of the motive, or by what method or who the intended may be or who is doing the killing. This would probably lead to another declaration: there are always situations when it is necessary to kill another human being, such as in the case of a war, in self-defense, to save the life of another or to end a loved one's suffering—or, even still, as punishment. This is a topic that is as old as life itself and can be debated endlessly by all sides. Some could even see it as a religious decision, an "eye for an eye" or "Thou shalt not kill." Others still may see it as a necessity to avenge a wrong for whatever twisted reason their mind may justify, and then, there is the oldest reasons of all, for love. This story will cover most, if not all, of those beliefs.

1

Two Mothers

You could have set your watch by the small quasi-military procession and timing of the night's event if you knew that it was a Thursday night or if you were lucky enough to be personally invited to sit in one of the four well-worn old oak church pews in the large, dimly lit execution chamber at the Big House on the Hudson River, in Ossining, New York. These pews were reserved for a select group of fourteen individual spectators who would, in a matter of a very few short minutes, become the hand-picked witnesses to a celebrated and scheduled event mandated by law. The only other seat in the spacious room was an oversized handcrafted dark oak seat for one, the electric chair. It was strategically placed in the middle of the large room just off the northeast wall, directly facing those chosen few people sitting in the four oak pews. Were the church pews a theogonist's statement to the event or were they just a utilitarian necessity?

The oversized oak seat was bolted to the floor and surrounded by a thick, grayish-green rubber floor covering. A thinner rubber of the same color covered the chair's back rest and seating area. Randomly placed brass spittoons were placed between the church pews for the fourteen onlookers—no smoking allowed. On Thursday nights, and only Thursday nights, at exactly 11:00 p.m., not a minute before or later, New York State's executioner would be present to fulfill his job description, which was to manually move a metal lever up and down three times, sending the required three separate electrical charges (a time-proven method) of a precise voltage into the body of the condemned human who sat strapped into that old oak chair not twenty feet away, and all according to law. At times, he'd have to move that lever up and down more than three times, if there were more than one execution scheduled for the night's events—the record is seven in one night. All New York executions were conducted by New York court-ordered death warrants, and they were carried out in New York's only electric chair.[1]

At the stroke of 11:00 p.m. on Thursday, January 21, 1932, Francis "Two Gun" Crowley solemnly shuffled through the open doorway at the northeast wall, slowly dragging his suede sleepers along the smooth but overused concrete floor, his short arms crossed in front at his waist. Escorted by five prison keepers (correction officers), few, if any, words were spoken by either Crowley or the keepers, and then only in an inaudible whisper. Absolute silence was mandatory for every one of the spectators. Crowley was dressed in the required execution clothing of a condemned prisoner. Dark gray pants, white shirt and suede prison slippers.[2] His short walk ended as he was positioned in front of the old handcrafted oak chair that displayed a ten-inch urine stain in the greenish-gray rubber tacked to the seat. The headrest bore scorch marks from the many prior human skulls' resistance to electricity. The wooden arms had been worn smooth by the thrashing of the condemned as the jolting current invaded their bodies. Two copper-tipped electrodes waited like coiled snakes on the rubber mat as the prison keepers prepared the two electrodes and leather restraints on the chair behind him. Crowley would have stood facing the four pews filled with the fourteen spectators.

Francis "Two Gun" Crowley's NYPD rogue's gallery arrest photo, taken in 1929 when he was eighteen years old, for grand larceny of an automobile. *Courtesy Yonkers PD.*

I'm sure he scanned the room, perhaps looking for a familiar face among them. But missing was that ever-present evil smirk that had so often lain across his cocky baby face; instead, his eyes were small and unemotional.[3] His small stature was dwarfed by the oversized oak electric chair, which measured just over four feet tall from ground level to the top of the backrest that patiently awaited him. Crowley stood at an arguable height of just barely five foot, three inches tall, on his tiptoes, and weighed not more than 110 pounds at his heaviest. His childlike feet dangled inches off the rubber-matted floor as he was guided into the chair, until the keeper strapped them into the wooden yoke at the base. He didn't project the image of a New York City gangster, let alone a notorious convicted cop killer.

To understand just how this young killer—who had just turned twenty years old less than three months earlier—could be standing, facing fourteen total strangers, some of whom had traveled long distances in New York's brutal January weather eagerly waiting to see him fry in that big oak electric chair, we'd have to go back to the beginning, to the latter part of the nineteenth century.

It all began back in 1890 on First Avenue, in a shabby, rundown tenement on the upper east side of Manhattan, with the birth of a girl named Dora Dietz. Dora's first name was really Dorothy, though she rarely if ever used that name. For the most part, or what is known of Dora, she was a typical child born to two German immigrant parents living a typical hardscrabble life in a Manhattan tenement, uneducated, but not without dreams. Dora was the third child of Peter and Elizabeth Dietz. Within the next twelve years, Dora would become a middle child, with the birth of a younger brother and sister, all living on First Avenue in a dilapidated Upper East Side tenement, a neighborhood of predominantly German immigrants. Both of Dora's parents appeared to be hardworking but never seemed to get ahead financially, or socially, as both struggled with the English language and lacked any formal education. Elizabeth, Dora's mother, was a homemaker with five children, while Peter, her father, was the family's financial provider. In 1902, tragedy struck the Dietz household with the unexpected death of Peter. Elizabeth struggled to provide for the youngest children, and the older ones, including Dora, though only about fourteen years old at the time, went to work.

Dora soon found a job as a housecleaner with Mr. and Mrs. Durege, who were also German immigrants living on the Upper East Side of Manhattan, but much better off financially, not far from Dora's mother's apartment.[4] Sometime in the early months of 1911, Dora met a twenty-four-year-old fella named John Flood. John was a single Irish immigrant working as a security guard for an elevated railroad company in New York City. He boarded with a couple other railroad security guards at the home of a New York City police officer named Patrick Leddy on 8th Avenue in Manhattan.[5] For an unknown reason, John Flood frequented the household where Dora worked. Unknown, because Dora's employer, Mr. Durege, was a music teacher, and what would be the reason Mr. Durege would have for a private security guard? Unless, of course, Flood had other talents. Either way, when Dora turned twenty-one years old, she found herself pregnant with John's child. When John learned of this, he not only refused to marry Dora but also didn't want anything to do with her, even when she looked to him for financial support. Dora was still living at home with her mother and perhaps burdened with the thought of becoming a single mother herself and the obligations to provide for a newborn. She had watched her mother struggle to get by, which must have had an enormous effect on Dora. She likely suffered the anxiety and embarrassment of being an unwed mother in the early part of the twentieth century, when a women's reputation was, at times, the only thing she could actually rely on for any type of improved social status if she was ever to break out of the slums. Dora must have realized that being abandoned like she had been by John Flood in her time of need, and for her to keep the child, to raise it on her own, was out of the question, as was an abortion. She must have also contemplated the concerns of the cultural demands on an unwed mother in 1911 and the loss of any dreams she may have had while still holding on to her self-respect as she made her decision.

On October 31, 1911, Dora Dietz gave birth to a son in a New York hospital and immediately handed him over to the Catholic Charities of New York.[6] Under a 1931 New York state law, an illegitimate child takes the name of his or her mother. But in this case, that wasn't necessary, as Dora gave the child up for adoption to the Catholic Charities and never looked back. Less than a year later, Dora married a German immigrant named Fred Schmidt and broke out of the overcrowded family tenement at 340 East 85th Street. For reasons that are unclear or remain unknown, Dora's marriage to Fred Schmidt was short-lived, and within a couple years, she was back in the tenement with her mother, sister and two brothers. By now, the youngest in the family was her nineteen-year-old sister, Roseanna. Dora was still using the last name of Schmidt while living in the Dietz family household. Years later, Dora referred to herself as a widow. Not exactly a lie, but it was likely an attempt to distance herself from any connection to the child she gave birth to on October 31, 1911, when questioned by a reporter.[7]

Sometime in the latter part of 1915, Dora met and married Walter Coleman, a steamfitter by trade, employed by Bethlehem Steel Company, and together they moved to Ravine Avenue in Yonkers, New York. Dora was finally out of the slums, again. Dora and Walter remained in Yonkers and had two children, and she became a stay-at-home mother. Early in 1930, Dora, Walter and their two children are forced to move back into Manhattan, to East 89th Street, the home of Dora's younger brother George Dietz. George was married with a two-year-old daughter, when his wife suddenly died after giving birth to their second child, a son, in early 1930. To help George care for his motherless children, Dora and her family remained with them well into the 1940s.[8] It's unknown if Dora ever acknowledged to her husband, Walter, or her children her past indiscretion and relationship with John Flood or that she gave birth to a son and placed him with Catholic Charities of New York. It is believed that she never did.

Within a short time, no more than two months or so after Dora gave birth to her illegitimate son, the child was fostered out by Catholic Charities of New York to a widow who also lived on the Upper East Side at 1838 3rd Avenue. The widow was Anna Crowley or Annie Crawley—depending on pronunciation, Crowley by the Kings English and Crawley if pronounced with a thick Irish brogue.[9] Anna listed her birthplace as England on her immigration papers, though it is believed that she was actually born in Ireland, sometime in or around 1873. Anna immigrated to the United States in 1889, when she was fifteen or sixteen years old.[10] In 1892, she met and married a fellow countryman from Ireland named Thomas. He was a hardworking bricklayer who immigrated to the United States in 1886 and was three years Anna's senior.[11] Together they made their home on 2nd Avenue in Manhattan. Within six years, the Crowleys had three children: a son named John, and two daughters, Mary and Margaret. In the early part of 1900, a third daughter, Sarah, was born, but she unexpectedly died in July of the same year.[12] Six years later, Anna's world was rocked again—only this time, it turned her life upside-down forever. Her bricklayer husband, Thomas, at only thirty-six years old, unexpectedly died in the Bronx.[13] Anna was left with three fatherless children to feed, clothe and shelter. She had no means of providing any of these necessary staples. She could read and write, but just barely. She had no occupation, or known talent, other than rising three babies.

By the end of 1911, Anna had been forced to move to the 3rd Avenue slums of the Upper East Side, where she soon learned to manage a very successful baby mill, thanks to Catholic Charities and other aid agencies in New York, some paying as much as seven dollars a week for the care of each child.[14] In a few short years, by 1915, Anna's baby mill had swelled; at times, as many as ten children were crammed into her overcrowded three-room tenement on 3rd Avenue, with the children's ages ranging anywhere from a newborn child to her own teenaged children. The revolving door of Anna's small apartment was busy, as Anna was struggling just to survive.[15] When Anna agreed to foster Dora's son from Catholic Charities, Dora had by that time moved on with her life, with no known plans of ever returning or taking custody of the child in the future. So, Anna, with the permission of Catholic Charities and without any legal adoption—but still maintaining a fostering agreement (for payment)—gave the child her last name, Crowley, with a first name of Francis.[16]

By 1920, Anna was nearing fifty years old, and the daunting task of rearing foster children must have been taking its toll, physically and mentally—not that she was known to be any good at fostering children or even caring for her own children.

Life wasn't easy during these times for immigrant women like Anna, much less in the crime-ridden, rundown, unsanitary tenement slums of New York. As the hardships of fostering children grew, Anna reduced the number of children to three. But most of the time, it was only two, as young Francis, who proved early on to be more than just a handful with his behavioral problems, had been removed from her care at the age of nine and placed in a children's asylum for behavioral issues.[17] Anna then moved to a fifth-floor tenement at 300 East 134th Street in the Bronx. Two of her own children were now in their early twenties, and they could provide some financial relief for Anna—when they weren't in jail.

Anna's biological son, John, also proved to be somewhat of a problem child. At the tender age of twelve, he was removed from Anna's care and sentenced to the New York Catholic Protectory for children in Westchester County, New York, due to his criminal behavior.[18] John would serve another two sentences there before he was nineteen years old for his behavioral issues and criminal activity.[19] Anna remained at the 300 East 134th Street address in the Bronx until November 14, 1927, when she was fifty-seven years old; that year, she married fifty-eight-year-old Mathew Kavanagh, a flagman for the railroad.[20] Together they moved out of the Bronx, to 134-26 231st Street in Laurelton, New York. Moving to Laurelton in Queens County must have been a welcome relief for Anna. For the most part, it was a rural setting, but still considered New York City proper. Laurelton is situated on the eastern edge of Queens County and borders on the western edge of Nassau County on Long Island.

With the aging newlyweds came Anna's oldest daughter, Helen Crowley, now twenty-eight years old; Francis Crowley, seventeen years old; and a sixteen-year-old boarder named John Denahy, who had been in Anna's foster care since he was a year old.[21] Francis never actually moved into the Laurelton location with Matthew Kavanagh and his new bride, but he did sleep there occasionally. Francis chose to spend most of his time bouncing around Manhattan, Harlem and the Bronx. The places he knew, where he was comfortable. Where he was hidden within the hustle and bustle of the city life, crowded surroundings, he could blend in and be invisible when he had to. He did, however, use Anna's new Laurelton address whenever he was arrested.[22]

Brother John

Francis Crowley's early foster years with Anna Crowley were anything but nurturing. It could very well be that he slipped through the cracks because of no real adult supervision, but it was more likely that he was just overlooked, lost in the shuffle. This may have not been so hard to do, with Anna's many foster children to tend to on a daily basis. He also appeared to have some physical and mental development challenges in his formative years. His size always seemed to be an issue; being the smallest in both height and weight for his age caused him constant anxiety in school and around other children his age. It could be contributed to the lack of a healthy nutritional environment, genetics or any number of birth-related issues based on the lifestyle of his birth mother and her environment, or the healthcare available to her during her pregnancy with him, if any. It could also be said that young Francis developed his own survival mechanism based on life as he was treated, adding to many of his personal identity scars. As a child, young Francis was introverted and shy, which caused him to be somewhat of a loner, rebellious and defensive.[23] His behavioral issues as a young child caused him to be removed from Anna's foster custody on five different occasions before the age of twelve, sometimes for lengthy periods of time.[24] After each instance, Anna would always take him back.

Anna testified at his murder trial that she enrolled young Francis in his first school at Saint Jerome's Elementary on Alexander Avenue in the Mott Haven section of the Bronx, not far from their 134th Street home. But it was short-lived, because Frank, as she called him, would always play hooky and didn't like the school.[25] Frank was expelled from Saint Jerome's and sent to the Sisters of Saint Dominic's home for children in Blauvelt, New York.[26] After his release, he was returned to Anna's foster care. She then enrolled him into the local public school, P.S. 43 on Brown Place in the Bronx, also in the Mott Haven section. Again, after a short time, he was removed for truancy and behavioral problems. This time, he was sent to Saint Michael's home for children in Staten Island. After a short stint, he ran away, back to Anna in the Bronx. By this time, Francis was around eleven or twelve years old, and he refused to go back to school. Had he chosen to return to school, any school, he most certainly would have felt out of place being placed in the grade level he had last attended, which was around the third grade.[27] Collectively, what little time Francis did spend in a school classroom was all but wasted; he couldn't read or write and was just barely able to scratch his name. About the time he turned twelve years old, he took a job in a local box factory, working for Monroe Dix, and shared what little money he made with Anna.[28] Anna maintained that Frank was a good boy, as she always took his earned money.[29]

Francis Crowley never knew or formally met his biological mother and father, and by all accounts, he never asked about them either. With one exception: when Francis Crowley was about fourteen years old, and only for a brief glance at a stranger, a woman visited Anna Crowley in their Bronx apartment. There was a brief visit with a short conversation between Anna and the unknown woman; their conversation tone was low, and Francis couldn't make out what they were saying. After the woman left, Francis asked Anna who the woman was, Anna then told him that it was his real mother, the one who gave him up to foster care. At this time, Anna briefed Francis on what little she knew about his biological father, that his name was John Flood and he was a policeman (a security guard to some, was also considered the police). Francis's only reply was in reference to his biological mother: "I don't care, I don't like her."[30]

With the absence of any adult man in Francis life, the only real close male he knew was John Crowley, Anna's biological son, whom Francis idolized and became attached to.[31] John was at least fourteen years older than Francis, and he was anything but a role model for anyone. In 1910, John was sentenced in New York's children's court to nine months in the Catholic Protectory in Westchester County, New York, for truancy. Other stays followed: in 1911, another three months for violation of his parole; in 1913, sentenced to fifteen months for another charge; in 1914, sentenced to three years for assault but paroled in 1915 (automatic under the law) because he was twenty-one years old. In 1915, John Crowley violated his parole again and was sentenced to another year. In June 1916, six days after his release, he was arrested for burglary, but his sentence was suspended. In January 1918, he was arrested for felony assault, but the grand jury failed to reach an indictment and he was released. In April 1918, he was sentenced to one year in Elmira Reformatory (Prison) for burglary. On December 13, 1921, he was indicted for first-degree murder for killing seventeen-year-old James L. Hayes on March 21, 1921, during a gang fight on East 100th Street. On December 29, 1922, the murder charge was dismissed; the only eyewitness went missing, but John was still held for a parole violation and sentenced to Elmira Reformatory again. Then he was released on December 27, 1924.[32]

Sometime during the short and sporadic periods of John Crowley's early years, those years that he remained at large, he managed to leave an indelible impression on young Francis Crowley. Though they weren't related by blood, they did share some of the same tangible realities of life and impoverished surroundings. To Francis, John was a great eminence; he taught Francis how to take the things he wanted from those who had the things he wanted. He taught him how to drive a car and how to hotwire and steal the car of his choice. Francis always referred to John Crowley as his brother.[33] John, also known as Jack Crowley, served nine terms in New York State prisons and was paroled seven times from almost every conceivable kind of institution, beginning when he was less than fourteen years old. So, it was no surprise then on the afternoon of January 15, 1925, somewhere around 3rd Avenue in New York City, when twenty-seven-year-old John Crowley was driving a taxicab in an erratic manner and stopped by New York City patrolman Maurice Harlow. Crowley was unable to produce a driver's license and appeared to be under the influence of alcohol. Once Crowley exited the taxicab, he became belligerent and refused to cooperate with Patrolman Harlow. The situation escalated, with Crowley grabbing Harlow's nightstick away from him and threatening to beat him with it. Patrolman Harlow was forced to pull his service revolver to gain control of Crowley and defuse the situation. Crowley was arrested and held overnight, but he was released the following day after paying a five-dollar fine. The whole episode caused Crowley to make a threat against the patrolman for getting in his way. Crowley stated that he would "get" Harlow and kill the next cop that got in his way.[34]

Shortly before 1:00 a.m. on the rainy Sunday morning of February 22, 1925, twenty-six-year-old New York City patrolman Maurice Harlow, shield no. 11181, of the Thirty-Ninth Precinct, was on foot patrol in the precinct

Left: John Crowley's NYPD rogue's gallery arrest photo as it appeared in the *New York Daily News* on Monday, February 23, 1925. *Courtesy of the* New York Daily News.

Right: Patrolman Maurice Harlow, shield no. 11181, World War I military photo. *Courtesy of the Library of Congress.*

and assigned by his command to respond to a loud party complaint at 1812 3rd Avenue, the home of Thomas F. Maher. Patrolman Harlow confronted Maher at his apartment about the noise complainant, and he was told to keep the partygoers quiet. But unbeknownst to Patrolman Harlow at the time, he was instantly recognized by one of the intoxicated guests inside the Maher apartment—it was none other than John Crowley. Under the influence of alcohol, resentment and his psychotic nature, Crowley quietly followed Patrolman Harlow as he left the Maher apartment, down the stairs and out of the building onto the street. Crowley's bride of just a couple weeks, Alice, who was also attending the party, followed close behind. As soon as Crowley exited 1812 3rd Avenue and was on the sidewalk, he looked down the quiet street and observed Patrolman Harlow with his back toward him, as he was just passing the entrance to the next apartment building in the rain. There were no known witnesses, or none who came forward anyway, other than the intoxicated twenty-five-year-old Alice, wife of John Crowley, who stated that it was Patrolman Harlow who attacked her husband, and John was just defending himself.

Detectives Joseph Malone, Joseph Mackle and John Cahill, all from Patrolman Harlow's precinct were able to piece together a synopsis of that fatal event based on the elementary applied physics of the physical evidence, plus a timeline established by Maher, the weapons used and a trail of spent cartridges from Crowley's gun. What actually occurred on that rainy, early morning in East Harlem between John Crowley and Patrolman Maurice Harlow, it is believed, is that when Crowley saw Patrolman Harlow walking down 3rd Avenue, Crowley pulled out his handgun and began to pursue Harlow at a fast pace. Though he was intoxicated, Crowley started shooting at Harlow as he ran toward the patrolman from behind. One of Crowley's first bullets struck the unsuspecting Harlow behind his left ear. Harlow's body wheeled around from the force of the bullet as he fell to the sidewalk, but just before he lost consciousness and died, he somehow managed to pull his revolver from its holster and fired two rounds, one hitting the fast-approaching Crowley in the stomach.

When police backup arrived, they found Crowley directly across the street, lying in the doorway of a building and bleeding from a single gunshot wound to his stomach, his new wife bent over him. Patrolman Harlow was lying dead on the pavement with his service revolver still clutched in his hand, a single bullet wound to the back of his head. Crowley was taken to Mount Sinai Hospital, and Alice, suffering from alcoholism and shock, was placed under arrest and held in the prison ward of Bellevue Hospital. Alice was also held as material witness, should her husband live. A three-year veteran of the NYPD, twenty-six-year-old Patrolman Maurice F. Harlow SH. 11181 was taken to his residence at 507 West 170th Street (which was the practice at the time), where his own new bride anxiously awaited his return. Just three weeks before, she was the gushing bride-to-be, May Coughlin, now the widow of NYPD patrolman Maurice Harlow. Patrolman Harlow was also a U.S. Army veteran of World War I.[35] John Crowley died within the week at Mount Sinai from Patrolman Harlow's well-placed and final shot. With that, Alice was released from custody.

With the shooting death of NYPD patrolman Maurice Harlow, the public demanded answers to how someone like John Crowley, with such an extensive criminal past and history of incarceration and parole, be allowed to freely walk the streets of New York. The New York State parole board's practice came under intense scrutiny, and the obvious weakness of the system was exposed. Dr. Frank Christian, the superintendent of Elmira

Reformatory, was quick to point out that John Crowley was pronounced by the psychiatrist who examined him upon his first admission to Elmira as an "incurable psychopathic delinquent who should be restrained for life." Dr. Christian also added:

> *This class of inmate (psychotic) individual who commit spectacular crimes are in the limelight for publicity. They are the ones who are featured on the front pages of the sensational press, their aim is to do something "big," and their ego must have an outlet. Whether they are in jail or at liberty.*[36]

With the sudden death of his mentor, the direct result of a policeman's bullet, young Francis Crowley fell deeper into his psychotic abyss of revenge, swearing to avenge his brother's death at all cost. His hatred of the police became the foremost excuse to carry on his criminal lifestyle, compounded only by the abandonment issues he suffered from his biological parents refusing to accept him. But perhaps the most repressed motivation of all was that his biological father was by all known accounts a policeman, or that's what he had been told. Crowley's life continued to falter from the weight of that enormous chip on his shoulder.[37]

By 1928, Crowley had reached his seventeenth birthday and his behavioral issues at his foster home began to fade, as he was no longer under the threat of being removed from Anna's care and sent to another children's asylum. It is also assumed at this point that Anna was no longer receiving foster care money from the Catholic Charities. Though Crowley was still living with Anna at 300 East 134th Street in the Bronx, he had for the most part taken to living off the street, fending for himself and plying his craft. He stole by whatever means available from the growing population of New York City, around six and a half million people by the early 1930s. Crowley liked to steal cars, a craft lovingly taught to him by John Crowley. For fun, Francis would steal a car in Manhattan and ditch it in Queens; then, to get back to Manhattan, he would steal a car in Queens and ditch it in Manhattan. It was a game to him, and he became very good at stealing cars, any make or model—plus, he liked to drive.[38]

Francis was so good at stealing cars that he began to get a reputation among the neighborhood gangs as the go-to guy when they needed a car. When a local gang leader came to him with an order to steal a car—and there were many gang leaders—it felt good to him; it was like he was being accepted as a specialist. Finally, he thought, someone needed something from him; it boosted his ego and gave him a purpose. Even if he wasn't accepted into the mainstream of their gang, they needed him for something. They even gave him a nickname, "Shorty," which he liked—so much so that he would even refer to himself at times as Shorty, never realizing it was a somewhat derogatory label.[39] Though his enlarged ego would later relate more with the criminal bravado name of "Two Gun," he could never hide from the media's descriptions of "Half Pint Murderer," "Boy Slayer" and "Midget Frank," to name a few.[40]

3

Taxi Dancers

On January 17, 1920, the Eighteenth Amendment to the U.S. Constitution went into effect as a nationwide prohibition to the manufacturing, importation, sale and transport of alcohol in the United States. First introduced in Congress and passed by both houses in December 1917, it wasn't until January 16, 1919, that the amendment had been ratified by thirty-six of the forty-eight states, making it law. Eventually, only two states, Connecticut and Rhode Island, opted out of ratifying it. On October 28, 1919, Congress passed the Volstead Act, named for the Minnesota congressman who introduced the legislation to enforce the Eighteenth Amendment. With that, a total of 1,500 federal Prohibition agents, called dry agents (now the Drug Enforcement Agency), were tasked with the enforcement of the new and mostly unpopular amendment. While the manufacture, importation, sale and transportation of alcohol was illegal in the United States, Section 29 of the Volstead Act allowed for wine and cider to be made from fruits at home, but not beer. Up to two hundred gallons of wine and cider could be made, with some people growing wine grapes for home use. The act did not prohibit consumption of alcohol, and many people stockpiled wines and liquors for their personal use in the latter part of 1919 before sale of alcohol beverages became illegal.

As a result of the Volstead Act, and its enforcement, the use and availability of alcohol was driven into the underground and controlled mainly by organized gangs, which some have attributed to the increase in crime in the urban areas of the country and the black-market violence that resulted from it. One thing was for sure, Prohibition had a profound effect on the music industry in the United States, specifically jazz. Unadvertised locations to drink and dance were called speakeasies, and they were popping up all over, extremely popular and abundant. As the unpopular amendment continued, so did the enforcement, especially selective enforcement. As early as 1925, it was believed that Prohibition was a complete failure and wasn't working. To some, it was assumed that Prohibition worked best when directed at its primary target: the working-class poor. A rich family could have a cellar full of alcohol and get by, but if a poor family had one bottle of home brew, there would be hell to pay. Working-class people were inflamed by the fact that their employers could dip into a private cache while they, the employees, could not. It was estimated that as many as 20,000 to 100,000 illegal speakeasies flourished in New York by the mid-1920s, hidden in the underground away from the dry agents of Prohibition.[41]

A young Francis Crowley watched from the shadows of the forgotten slums in the filthy crime-ridden streets of the Upper East Side and the Bronx in an overcrowded three-room baby mill run by a single, uneducated, Irish immigrant foster mother. She was well in over her head with just trying to get by. Her added responsibility of caring for so many foster children only added to the forthcoming results of an emotionally unstable and toxic youth. Crowley lived a life resentful of any structured authority. He was being nurtured by daily events on the dark side of life compared to those enjoying the fruits of the Roaring Twenties.[42]

Crowley's resentment of authority was magnified again in late 1927, when Anna got married to Matthew Kavanagh, and in 1928, they moved away from the Bronx, away from the only home and mother he had ever associated himself with. His hostilities to authority deepened, as his abandonment issues forced him farther out into life on the streets and on his own.[43] In early 1929, Anna somehow managed to persuade her son-in-law Timothy J. Doherty, who ran a successful wire lathe business out of the Mott building at 41 Lexington Avenue in Manhattan, to hire Crowley as a wire lather. He joined the Metal Lathers Union, Local No. 46.[44] Lathers were in the building trade; they fastened wood, metal or rock board lath on to walls, ceilings and partitions to provide a supporting base for plaster. It was never revealed, either through interviews with family members or court testimony, whether Crowley had actually taken to the trade.

However, it is known that the stock market crash of October 24, 1929, which was only a few months after he began as a lather, devastated the building industry in the country. The crash would have had a direct result

An early 1931 illegal still operation being dismantled in Merrick, New York, by Nassau County detectives and a uniformed patrolman from the NCPD First Precinct. *Courtesy Nassau County PD.*

mostly unfavorable to someone like Crowley, who was most probably in an apprenticeship with his new position. Doherty was the husband of Anna's biological daughter Mary, who also lived in Laurelton, Queens. This new position as a lather came only after Crowley lasted one month as an office boy at the Walcott Printing Company on East 25th Street in Manhattan.[45] As an office boy, Crowley was earning $15 a week, but he gloated at earning $65 a week as a union lather. This was a handsome wage for anyone at that time, especially for a sixteen- or seventeen-year-old.[46] In today's world, given the rate of inflation, that would be around $2,000 a week. This would be a remarkable amount of money and an honest living for a guy who couldn't read or write, resented any type of organized structure by any authority figure and liked to steal cars. In 1929, Crowley was arrested on four different occasions for grand larceny, all for stealing cars. These were just the times he was actually caught, once in Queens County, once in Manhattan, and twice in the Bronx—all the cases were dismissed.[47] This may have only energized his taste for stealing. For someone who had boasted that he was good at stealing cars, 1929 must have just been an off year for him. Though his police records don't provide the actual circumstances for these arrests, Crowley would later state that he always took a good shellacking (beating) from the police every time he was arrested[48] and that the courts had placed him on lifetime parole and ordered to stay out of the Bronx.[49] Which he didn't.

By February 1931, nineteen-year-old Francis "Two Gun" Crowley's life was nearing out of control. The stock market crash on October 24, 1929 (known as Black Tuesday), which created a devastating economic ripple effect across the entire country, then across the globe, ushered in the Great Depression. First it was the stocks, and then the worldwide GPD fell by an estimated 15 percent. By comparison, the worldwide gross domestic product (GDP) fell by less than 1 percent in the 2008–9 recession. An estimated fifteen million Americans were unemployed. The Depression had a devasting effect on both the rich and the poor, with inflation reaching between 25 and 33 percent.[50] This meant that even if you were lucky enough to have a job, the inflation rate wiped out any purchasing power your salary once had. Many of those who stood in the long soup lines for one meal a day were still employed, but they couldn't afford to eat and feed their families. Those who did have jobs couldn't count on their longevity, especially in the building sector. The Great Depression lasted until the beginning of World War II.[51]

By all accounts, the Great Depression had little effect on Crowley, save for maybe now he had to do two or three stickups (robberies) to get the money he gotten before in only one holdup. In some ways, he actually benefited from the recession; most urban Americans had a complete and total distrust for the banking industry, especially after the Federal Reserve allowed some large public banks to fail and remain in business. Many working-class Americans rushed to their banks, only to be turned away, and found that they had lost all their hard-earned savings. This was just the beginning of lower middle-class Americans being pushed further into the depths of poverty and all the personal hardships that came with it. Though most hardworking citizens were law abiding, they didn't find it too taxing to look the other way when some thug or thugs robbed a bank.[52] There were times when they actually rooted for the bad guys over the police, especially those who robbed a bank or banks. It was like a proxied revenge, more so as the Great Depression worsened and money became harder to come by.[53] Many more carried what little cash they had on their persons or stuffed it under a mattress at home rather than trust a bank. But they didn't factor into account guys like Crowley, who preyed on that belief and fear. Or if they did, it was a risk worth taking.

The Depression also created a few jobs as well, especially in urban environments with large numbers of tenements and apartment dwellers. One such job was that of rent collector. Rent collectors worked exclusively for the building owners, many of whom were of questionable (thuggish) character themselves, though no match for the midget killer, with his guns in their face. The rent collector would receive a small fee to collect and record the rent money (always in cash) from each tenant in a particular apartment building, saving the building owner from making the threats of eviction to the dweller or exposing themselves to personal harm because of those threats. Rent collectors were as popular as bank managers. So, at the beginning of each month, the rent collector would physically knock on each and every apartment door, collecting the rent for that particular month, plus any back-rent he could threaten or muscle out of the poor tenant. Crowley liked rent collectors, though. They were an easy mark for his quick stickups, and the police were always unable to find a witness. Clever Crowley always took the month's rent records along with the cash, leaving the tenant with a sympathetic (prove I didn't pay the rent) story for the building owner. It was like a quid pro quo of sorts for guys like Crowley.[54] In his written statement to Nassau County detectives Closs and Quinn, Crowley stated that sometime around the first of February 1931, he stuck up two rent collectors on 134th Street in the Bronx because he needed money to go to Philadelphia to buy some more guns. He further claimed that he received a total of about seventy dollars between both robberies. Crowley then stole a car and drove to Philadelphia, where he purchased two automatic handguns. Crowley boasted that "a person could buy anything in Philadelphia, any kind of gun, brass knuckles, blackjacks or knifes, all you needed was money." He also said that while the gun dealer was waiting on him, he skillfully managed to steal three additional guns from the dealer, and if the salesman had caught him stealing, he would have knocked him over the head.[55]

Other notable aspects to Francis "Two Gun" Crowley are that not only would he become a convicted cold-blooded psychopathic killer but he was also a clever, forward-thinking killer. He could be manipulative when he needed to be and a convincing liar when he felt the need to bolster his narcissistic ego. He would lie to anyone, whether he thought it was necessary or not.[56] In addition to his choirboy appearance, Crowley could conveniently manipulate other like-minded individuals with his bravado, aspirations and the tall tales of his past criminal accomplishments.[57] At times, he could even convincingly swing the police or draw in some unsuspecting innocent young girl with his own act of shy innocence. Crowley's speech was mildly impaired by a self-conscious stutter, though he learned to live with the slight but noticeable impairment. It was nevertheless another identity scar, perhaps the result of an abnormally thick tongue. He also found an object of sorts, in an effort to conquer all of his insecurities, something that would elevate him above all others, and that was the gun. So, in his mind, he thought that if a gun was the platform to equality, then two guns must be the supreme authority. It also appeared that whatever the conversation, to whomever he spoke, whether it was the police or some young girl he wanted to impress, Crowley would eventually turn on his self-proclaimed bravado.[58]

So, it was around this time after Anna and her new husband, Matthew Kavanagh, moved out of the Bronx to Queens that Crowley started to frequent certain entertainment establishments around Harlem and Manhattan. Though he didn't drink or smoke, so he said—and his mother testified to that fact—he also didn't have Anna or her two daughters to keep tabs or control of him, not that they could.[59] So, at night, he started going around to the taxi dance halls to meet girls. Crowley didn't have a lot going for himself. He was extremely shy, almost introverted, and self-conscious of his stature. His speech was marred by the slang of the slums; he wasn't a prospect for any decent girl. Therefore, he started hanging around the taxi dance halls in Harlem.

Taxi dance halls could be traced back to somewhere around the days of the Barbary Coast of San Francisco, which evolved from the California gold rush days of 1849. They were frequented by gold prospectors and sailors from all over the world. Back then, they were called Barbary Coast dance halls. Within these dance halls, female employees danced with male patrons and earned their living from paid commissions, paid by the drinks they could encourage their male dance partners to buy. By the early twentieth century, this had evolved into a system of dance academies, where customers could buy a token that entitled them to one dance with a female employee. Some people used this as a way to learn how to dance or to learn new popular dances. This system then spread across the county, from California, to Chicago and finally to New York, becoming popular in the summer of 1919.

This system became so popular that the dance academies in New York quickly spread to an increasing number of noninstructional dance halls, where the dancers typically received half of the ticket price as wages and the other half paid for the overhead of the dance hall and the orchestra. By 1931, taxi dance halls flourished in the larger cities of United States, with an estimated over one hundred taxi dance halls in New York city alone, patronized by between thirty-five and fifty thousand men every week. Possibly the most popular of all New York taxi dance halls was the Orpheum, located at 46th Street and Broadway, which remained open for almost fifty years.

Taxi dance halls were feasibly the only way a socially awkward man could actually meet and interact with a talented pretty girl. Almost forgotten today, the taxi dancer was a famous type, spawning not only the 1930 hit song by Richard Rodgers of the Rodgers and Hammerstein fame but also the 1931 Columbia picture *Ten Cents a Dance* starring Barbara Stanwyck and directed by Lionel Barrymore. However, these taxi dance halls soon came under increasing attack by reform movements that deemed some dance halls outright dens of iniquity, populated mainly by charity girls (otherwise known as prostitutes).[60]

In the 1992 movie *A League of Their Own*, Madonna's character mentions that if the league folds, "she refuses to go back to taxi dancing, having guys sweating gin on her for ten cents a dance will never happen again." Generally, and for the most part, the taxi dancers of New York in 1931 were young, attractive, usually single women between the ages of fifteen and twenty-eight—although some dancers were undoubtedly older. The taxi dancer profession skewed toward the young and single. A majority of the young girls came from homes in which there was little or no financial support from the father. Occasionally, dancers were runaways, and many more came from homes where the parents were separated. Despite their relatively young ages, a sizable number of the dancers had been previously married. Many were immigrants from European countries such as Poland, Sweden, the Netherlands, Germany and France.

Some, if not all, of the dancers adopted aliases so that their activities might not become known to their families, as the cultural issues created conflict between the young taxi dancers and their families.[61] The term *taxi dancer* comes from the fact that, as with a taxicab driver, the dancer's pay is proportional to the time she spends dancing with the customer—the more time, the more money. Patrons in a taxi dancehall typically purchased tickets for ten cents each, which gave rise to the phrase "dime-a-dance girl." Other names for taxi dancers are *dance hostess* or *nickel hopper*, which gained popularity in the United States because out of each dime, the taxi dancer would typically keep five cents.

Tickets weren't only sold individually; a patron could purchase a book of twelve tickets for around $1.10 or $1.15 depending on the dance hall and its advertised special rates. A typical dance would last less than two minutes, and the patron would then have to give the dancer another ticket for another dance. Or, if the patron really liked the dancer, he might just give her a book of twelve tickets and occupy her time for twelve dances, whether they danced or just talked. This was standard practice if the patron was sweet on a particular dancer. It could also be encouraged by the dancer herself if she was sweet on the patron and looking beyond dancing for the rest of her life. More times than not, the patron would be trying to arrange a date with the dancer for a meeting after the dance hall closed for the night, not looking for a long-term commitment.[62] Prostitution and alcohol were not uncommon in some of the seedier taxi dance halls of New York, which attracted an undesirable element.[63]

4

Fats

It was in the Primrose Dance Club on West 125th Street and 7th Avenue in Harlem—which Crowley frequented almost nightly—that he found his partner in crime. To the casual observer, it wouldn't seem like Francis Crowley and Rudolph Duringer shared anything in common, let alone would die in the same manner. Duringer was seven years older than Crowley, almost a foot taller and more than one hundred pounds heavier—a real Mutt and Jeff duo.[64] Duringer was a truck driver from the town of Ossining, in Westchester County, on the northern border to the Bronx. Rudolph was known as Rudy to his friends in Manhattan, but in Ossining, he was called "Fats," short for Fatty Arbuckle, a popular comedian of the '20s and '30s.[65] Duringer, the only child of Anna and Charles Duringer, grew up on the West Side of Manhattan. The family first lived on West 125th Street but moved to West 128th Street. His mother, Anna, stayed at home, while his father, Charles, worked at a couple different jobs, first as a salesman for a milk company and eventually ending up as a truck driver. Like many other households at the time, the Duringers took in boarders to supplement Charles's income. Rudolph wasn't necessarily a problem growing up—he was just lazy.[66] His mother would later state that he had never been in any trouble with the law. As a child, he was labeled a bully by other schoolkids, which may not have actually been true. There seems to be some indication that he was somewhat mentally slow, or dimwitted, a common term used back in the 1930s, and he may have been just defending himself from the actual bullies. Either way, in his

Rudolph Duringer, also known as Fats, Rudy and Red. *Courtesy Yonkers P.D.*

teen years, his parents moved him out of the city and sent him to live with Anna's sister Catherine Kramm and her husband, William, at 12 Broad Avenue in Ossining.[67]

By all accounts, Duringer was a reliable and trusted truck driver living with his aunt and uncle in Ossining; he gave no trouble to them or anyone else. There is even some evidence that at times he made deliveries to the Sing Sing Prison; at other times, on specific Friday mornings, he made body pickups from the back door of the prison's death chamber. One thing is known for sure, and that is Fats liked to eat, and he ate a lot. He was also a heavy drinker. Perhaps he could even be classified as a functioning alcoholic, though not so functioning all the time.[68]

Crowley spent many of his nights hanging around the Primrose Dance Club, though he would periodically search out other dance halls or places where he could meet girls and cause his share of trouble. One such place was the Harry C. Wilson American Legion Post No. 762, located at 275 Bonner Place, tucked away on a quiet side street off 135th Street in the Bronx. One Sunday night, February 22, 1931, the American Legion was hosting a George Washington birthday celebration dance, and all things seemed to be going well. The dance had ended, and the patrons all left. The Legion members were inside cleaning up the hall, when sometime around 4:45 a.m. a member received a complaint from a couple of neighbors about the rowdy noise occurring outside on the Legion property, a spillover from the dance they thought, and no doubt fueled by alcohol. So, two veterans, John Waters and Harry Linzer, went outside to quiet the noise, and a fight broke out with the four noisemakers. During the altercation, both Waters and Linzer, who were unarmed, were shot by one of their four assailants. Waters was shot through both calves, and Linzer was shot once in the right thigh with a .25-caliber automatic. The perpetrators were all from a local gang and fled before the police arrived. Harry Linzer and John Waters were taken to the Morrisania Hospital by ambulance. The police later identified their attackers as John Byrne of 241 East 207th Street, Thomas Cullen of 372 East 138th Street and Gerald Weed of 8 West 181st Street, all from the Bronx, and Francis Crowley of 124–28 231st Street in Laurelton,

Queens. Crowley was identified as the lone shooter. Waters and Linzer would later recover from their gunshot wounds.[69]

NYPD detective Ferdinand "George" Schaedel, shield no. 76 of the Forty-Second Squad, Eighteenth Detective Division, was the lead detective in the investigation of the shooting at the American Legion post. As a result of Schaedel's investigation, John Byrne was arrested at the Lincoln Hotel on 136th Street in the Bronx, where he had shared a room with Crowley by Detectives Schaedel and Barry. Byrne was also in possession of a loaded revolver at the time of his arrest. A uniformed policeman had already arrested Gerald Weed during the commission of a robbery within the confines of the Thirty-Fourth Precinct. Thomas Cullen was arrested by Detectives Schaedel and Barry on March 7, 1931, but subsequently released when the victims failed to identify him as one of the combatants when they were shot. Crowley remained at large.[70]

Detective Schaedel continued his hunt for the last of the four and found that Crowley was a member of the lathers' union and was sometimes employed by Timothy Doherty, whose business, Ferro Building Products Inc., was located at 369 Lexington Avenue, in the Mott Building on the nineteenth floor, suite 1901. Sometime around the beginning of the second week in March 1931, Detective Schaedel made contact with Doherty and informed him of the events from February 22 and that Crowley was wanted in that shooting. An arrangement was made between Detective Schaedel and Doherty for Doherty to lure Crowley to his office the following Friday at 4:00 p.m. so Detective Schaedel could take him into custody. At 3:50 p.m. that Friday, Detective Schaedel arrived at Doherty's office ten minutes early to surprise Crowley when and if he showed. A short time later, an unsuspecting Crowley swaggered into Doherty's office. Detective Schaedel surprised Crowley, quickly pulled his service revolver and told him to put his hands up, he was under arrest. With that, Detective Schaedel removed a loaded .32-caliber Colt automatic from Crowley's waistband, and then secured his own service revolver in its holster.

Thinking that he had disarmed Crowley, Detective Schaedel secured the seized automatic into his coat pocket and turned the pint-sized criminal around to handcuff his hands behind him. Suddenly, Crowley bent over, pulling his hands free from Schaedel's grip. With his freed right hand, Crowley pulled another hidden automatic pistol from inside his coat pocket and, still in a bent-over position, fired three shots up between his outspread legs into Detective Schaedel's groin and stomach. Detective Schaedel fell to the floor, but he managed to get off two shots at Crowley as he fled the

NYPD photo of Detective Ferdinand "George" Schaedel, shield no. 76, of the Forty-Second Squad, Eighteenth Detective Division. *Courtesy NYPD.*

office and down the building's staircase. Both of Schaedel's shots missed, and he struggled to his feet to give chase. Bleeding profusely, Detective Schaedel dragged himself onto an elevator, and the operator, Robert Wilson, sped it straight down to the lobby. When the doors opened, Detective Schaedel called out to the proprietor of the lobby's cigar store, Max Cooper, who alerted a passing patrolman to call headquarters. The responding police blocked off Lexington Avenue at 41st Street, the adjoining side street, and conducted an office-by-office search throughout the twenty-six-story office building for Crowley. But he had eluded the police again. Thus, he earned the moniker "Two Gun" Crowley.[71]

Earlier that day, at about 10:00 a.m., Crowley, accompanied by four unidentified men, entered the Huguenot Trust Company branch on South Street in New Rochelle, New York. Pulling up to the curb in front of the bank in a blue or dark green sedan, one man entered the bank and began to prepare a deposit slip. A couple minutes later, he was joined by four additional men. One drew a sawed-off shotgun from beneath his coast while the others drew handguns. They order the four employees, three men and one woman, to go behind the counter and to keep their hands high in the air. Two of the holdup men emptied the cash drawers while another took several bundles of cash from the safe. Then four of the robbers leisurely walked out of the bank to their curbside vehicle while the fifth man covered their retreat. The total take from this bank robbery was $1,400.[72]

Crowley officially added cop shooter to his ever-expanding criminal repertoire, and he became the subject of a massive citywide police hunt. He knew he had to stay out of the Bronx, and he knew the police had his mother's address covered out in Laurelton. But he wasn't ready to leave the city, and he wasn't afraid of the police, but he had to keep moving around. After spending so many nights at the Primrose in Harlem, he became close with a dancer named Vera (Billie) Dunn, who was about twenty years old, five feet, six inches tall and around 135 pounds. According to the hardboiled NYPD detectives Dominik Caso and William Mara of the Forty-Second Detective Squad (the same squad as wounded Detective Schaedel), after Crowley shot Schaedel, Crowley and Dunn started moving around the city together, first staying at the Hudson River Apartments at 320 West 96th Street in no. 51. They lived there from March 11 to the end of March under the name Duffy. Then on April 1, they moved to the third floor of a furnished house at 239 East 14th Street in Manhattan under the name of Duff. A short time later, they moved again to 133 West 84th Street and stayed there until April 28. Abraham Subin, the building proprietor of 133 West 84th, stated that when they left his place, they had a total of four suitcases and stole his portable Atwater Kent radio. Billie Dunn was further described as having bobbed brown hair and three changes of dress: one black silk dress with short sleeves, a green afternoon dress and one white satin blouse with a blue skirt. Dunn also wore a flashy scarf tied in a bow knot over her left shoulder. Detectives Caso and Mara also learned that Crowley had been using the aliases Tommy Jordan, Francis Duffy, Tommy Duff and Tommy Dunn and was sometimes called Shorty.[73] Crowley managed to stay just ahead of Caso and Mara, and after April 28, the detectives lost his trail—though they wouldn't stop looking.

Crowley kept himself busy doing drugstore stickups and car thefts as he roamed around the city. He even robbed Howards Clothing store on 161st Street and took five new suits and $280 in cash, while Billie Dunn danced at the Primrose Club for nickels.[74]

On Wednesday evening, April 15, 1931, Crowley and two of his unidentified criminal acquaintances descended on the home of a wealthy real estate owner at 133 West 80th Street, only four short blocks from where Crowley and Billie were hiding out from the law. Rudolph Adler lived in the basement apartment of his building with his wife, Irene, and dog Trixie. Irene wasn't home when Crowley and his two friends came knocking, which was a good thing, just Rudolph and Trixie. After gaining entry, Crowley and his friends were disappointed that they couldn't find the trove of riches that they had been led to believe Adler hoarded in his basement. As frustration mounted, coupled with Trixie's aggressive behavior and her persistent barking at the three criminal intruders, Crowley unnecessarily, and coldheartedly, fired

Francis "Two Gun" Crowley NCPD arrest photo, 1931. *Courtesy Nassau County PD.*

five .32-caliber bullets directly into Rudolph Adler's chest. They fled empty-handed to an awaiting car with Trixie in hot pursuit.[75]

Working as a metal lather, if he was called to work, and if he showed, wasn't his kind of work. He found it was a lot easier to pull a five-minute job than work ten hours a day; plus, he liked stickups more. Though he did admit to studying the building trade to some extent, he was more interested to learn that some employers paid their workers in cash. The inside information that a certain construction foreman paid his workers in cash on Friday afternoons, and the route the foreman took to the job site, came in handy. Crowley knew the foreman, but the foreman didn't know Crowley, so while the foreman was standing on a crowded subway platform at 42nd Street one April Friday afternoon, Crowley walked up behind him, pushed a gun into his back and demanded the bag he was carrying, ordering him not to turn around or he would be shot. The foreman reluctantly, but wisely, passed the package back to Crowley without ever turning around, and Crowley was now $1,100 richer.[76]

What Detectives Caso and Mara didn't know was that Billie Dunn was a taxi dancer at the Primrose Club and could be found there most nights. If they waited around long enough, Crowley would eventual appear there as well. While Billie was making her easy money as a dancer, her boyfriend Francis was out with his new friend Fats Duringer speakeasy hopping and looking for the next person or place to rob. One night around the middle of April, Crowley went to a garage on 5th Street in Manhattan, stole a Packard sedan and drove it up to Ossining to meet Duringer. But Crowley wrecked the Packard in Ossining and had to steal a Chrysler sedan so he and Duringer could get back to cruising around the city and to the Primrose Club. Crowley had Duringer switch the license plates on the stolen Chrysler Imperial in an effort to go undetected if they were to be stopped by the police. So Duringer put the license plates from his own car, one that he sold a few days before, on the newly stolen Chrysler sedan, and off they went to Harlem. Duringer liked spending his time at the Primrose Club because he had just met a new dancer there and had fallen madly in love with her.[77]

5

Virginia "Joyce" Brannen

Virginia Cathleen Brannen was born on January 8, 1908, in Arlington, Massachusetts, to Joseph and Margaret O'Neil Brannen. Originally from Maine, Joseph was a carpenter by trade and employed by the local railroad. His wife, Marguerite, who went by Margaret, was originally from Canada. Virginia was their second of seven children, and shortly after her birth, they moved from Massachusetts back to Bangor, Maine, where Joseph and Margaret settled in at 131 2nd Street to raise their growing family. Joseph was a hardworking railroad employee, and Margaret was a busy stay-at-home mother.[78] From all reports, Virginia's life in Bangor was unremarkable; as the oldest daughter, she would have been expected to help her mother with the household chores and caring for her younger siblings. Virginia's education stopped at the eighth grade, as did that of a lot of children of that era.[79] As the family grew, Virginia's time was needed less and less at home. It's not exactly clear when Virginia actually left her parents' home to venture out into the world on her own, but it is reported that she remained in Bangor until she was twenty-three years old and worked at Gregory's Restaurant on Main Street.[80] Although Virginia wasn't living at home, she did contribute some of her earnings to her large family, This support didn't stop when she and her close friend from Bangor, Gertrude McDonald, took the giant leap from the quiet, laid-back lifestyle they lived in Maine and headed straight into the jaws of the fast-paced uncertainty of New York City. By all accounts, Virginia, who was known by Joyce to her friends in Bangor, was a good, responsible, caring daughter who secretly

Virginia Catherine Brannen, aka "Joyce." *Courtesy Yonkers PD.*

craved a more exciting life and was more than a little naïve.[81]

Virginia's mother knew of her plan to go to New York, although she was reluctant as a mother would normally be, knowing that her oldest daughter was heading off on her own to a strange city. She was also aware that Virginia, being a twenty-three-year-old single woman, wanted more out of life than what appeared available in Bangor. So, she gave Virginia her approval. Virginia's parents even arranged for her to board at the home of an old family friend, Alice Perro, with whom they had stayed in touch from their days back in Massachusetts and who had since relocated to the Bronx. Alice lived with her husband, William, a baker at a cracker factory, and their five children at 383 East 136th Street? in the Bronx.[82] Joseph Brannen would later tell the Bangor police that Virginia had left Bangor sometime in March to meet up with her childhood friend Gertrude in New York City. Gertrude had been in living in New York for some time before inviting Virginia to come to live and work with her. In fact, the year prior, Virginia had visited Gertrude in New York when Gertrude was working as a taxi dancer at the Golden Gate Dance Pavilion in Manhattan.[83] The thought of working as a taxi dancer was exciting to Virginia, and it came with a good salary; she could send more money home and meet new people. By this time, Gertrude had left the Golden Gate and was dancing at the Primrose Club, where she was instrumental in getting Virginia a job. Even though Virginia had no prior experience as a taxi dancer, with Gertrude's help, she was hired at the Primrose Club.[84] The naïve, cheerful twenty-three-year-old country girl from Maine was unaware that the Primrose Dance Club was just outside the boundaries of respectability and harbored a wide array of characters like Francis "Two Gun" Crowley and Fats Duringer.[85]

Virginia started off slow at the Primrose Club, but within a month it appeared that she was determined to make a go of it as a dancer. Plus, it was a close commute to Alice's home, just over the Willis Avenue bridge into the Bronx, and she was staring to make a about thirty dollars a week, enough so she could send five dollars a week home to her parents. She was making some new friends, and the excitement of city life hadn't worn off, yet.[86] One new friend was Fats Duringer, and the other was Francis "Two Gun" Crowley. Duringer treated Virginia really good; he threw a lot of dance tickets her way. He rarely danced with her through; his hulking, ill-shaped body and clumsy movements prevented him from being a good dance partner. Most of the time he was too drunk to dance anyway, but he liked Virginia because she paid attention to him, even if he did buy a lot of her dance time.[87] Duringer thought he was being treated extra special because Virginia thought he was an extra-special fella. He had never had a pretty girl like Virginia give him so much of her undivided time, and he was falling in love with her.[88] Duringer soon began to neglect his truck driving job and spend all his time at the Primrose Dance Club or out with his new friend Francis Crowley doing stickups or just eating. But whatever activity he was doing, he was doing it mostly intoxicated.[89]

In the early morning hours on Monday April 27, 1931, as the Primrose was closing its doors for the night, a few of the male patrons mingled around the sidewalk outside of the entrance, waiting for dancers they had successfully made earlier arraignments with. Mildred Moore would later testify as a witness in the murder trial at the Bronx Supreme Court that just before the Primrose doors closed, and before the orchestra stopped for the night, Fats Duringer had approached the cashier window; he was waiting for Virginia to finish up for the night. Then he reached into his pocket and took out a pile of silver and said to the cashier, "Shoot the works on tickets for Virginia." Moore said she wasn't sure how much he tossed away, but she was sure it wasn't less than two dollars. Moore would also testify that when the doors to the club closed, Virginia ran out and jumped into the backseat of a car, where Fats was sitting waiting for her. Moore would go on to state that Virginia was awful glad to see Fats; she was in good spirits and glad she was finished dancing for the night because it had been a busy one.[90]

Mildred Moore, who was also known as Mildred Armstrong, was a twenty-three-year-old blond party girl from the Bronx and the current girlfriend of Robert LeClair. Mildred was also a taxi dancer at the Primrose Club, though she preferred to party, but she did like to dance, just not for money. Not much is known about Mildred's life before the murder or after the trial except that at some time she was, or had been, married to a fella named Armstrong and was separated from him. As she was now seeing Robert LeClair, at times she would switch off using either name, Moore or Armstrong.[91] Robert LeClair was the same age as Mildred but a couple years older than Crowley; he was born on July 8, 1908, to Mary LeClair, a single mother living at 103 West 163rd Street in the Bronx. Even though he was older than Crowley, their lives paralleled in some ways. Robert was given up to the Charlestown orphanage in New York's Westchester County when he was about ten years old by his mother for reasons that remain unclear. However, he did return to his mother's house sometime around his eighteenth birthday.[92] By this time Mary LeClair had taken in a boarder by the name of James Skelly, and they married in 1934.[93] Robert never appeared to have any real behavioral issues or trouble with the law, but he did seem to be a little introverted, shy and gawky at times. He wore thick lens eyeglasses with dark frames that gave him that socially inept appearance, and when he wasn't working, he hung around the Primrose Club. LeClair worked as a metal lather and was a member of Local #46, where he had previously met Crowley. The older man was easily being led around by Crowley.[94] Again, it was somewhat of a clash in personalities between Robert's introverted shyness and Mildred's outgoing partying, and it all stemmed from the Primrose Club. On this particular night, when Virginia jumped into the backseat of that stolen Chrysler sedan with Fats Duringer—Mildred and Robert squeezed into the front seat with the driver, Francis "Two Gun" Crowley—she could not have known what was about to happen. Three of the four were highly intoxicated, as they later

Saint Joseph's Seminary wall where Duringer and Crowley dumped Virginia's lifeless body after Duringer shot and killed her. View is from curbside on Valentine Street. *Courtesy Yonkers PD.*

stated; only Crowley was sober, or less intoxicated than the others.[95] Witness statements made to the police and later court testimony provide a somewhat acceptable account of the tragic incident that occurred inside that stolen sedan in the early morning hours of Monday April 27, 1931.[96]

As daylight broke over the tranquil private estate of Saint Joseph's Seminary on quiet Valentine Street in Yonkers, a local workman walking along the road's edge observed the body of a woman wedged between the seminary's wall and the hedges that blocked the view of the buildings. The worker called to a nearby delivery wagon driver, who in turned called the police. Yonkers police chief Edward Quirk and a squad hurried to the scene and found a white female with a single gunshot wound to the chest. The police quickly determined that the woman had been dead for a very short time, perhaps less than an hour or two, as her body was still warm, but theorized she had been killed elsewhere and dumped at this location.

Her physical features were that of a woman in her early twenties: five feet, one inch, 115 pounds, medium build, with henna-colored hair (her natural hair color was dark brown, but she had added a slight reddish tint), blue eyes and a fair complexion. She wore a dark blue spring coat with a dress of a lighter blue and had on gray stockings but only one brown suede shoe.[97] Later examination of her body by Dr. Amos O. Squire, the Westchester County medical examiner, revealed she had been shot once at close range with a small-caliber bullet, just below the left breast, with the bullet exiting out her back. Further examination revealed she had vaccination scars on her upper left arm, and three false upper teeth—two incisors and one left lateral attached to a bridge—and no further signs of trauma. Her handbag was found near her body, though it contained very little information on initial inspection, and nothing found inside could immediately identify the body. One item of interest in the dead woman's handbag was a prescription drug bottle from a Maine doctor, filled at a local Bangor drugstore.[98]

The Bangor police were notified by the Yonkers PD by teletype with the description of the unidentified female and the details on the prescription bottle. (Teletype was a secure communication system between all police departments that was used for a wide variety of information or notifications. Messages could be directed to either one agency or multiple agencies nationwide. Any request or notification would be typed on a keyboard and sent via telephone lines to a particular police agency or nationwide. Most police departments and all New York precincts had the familiar 24/7 background noise of the rapid, short bursts of a loud mechanical typewriter stamping out messages on the large floor-mounted teletype machines. If a request or notification was intended for, say, one particular precinct or department, a bell would ring on that particular teletype machine indicating the incoming message should be read immediately.)

As this lead was being followed up with the Bangor police chief Thomas I. Crowley (no relation to Two Gun), Chief Quirk, Lieutenant Ford and the other detectives from the Yonkers PD pursued the other items found in the dead woman's handbag. One common practice during the Prohibition era was for speakeasies to hand out establishment cards, an advertisement of sorts, like today's business card. The handbag contained a few assorted cards from the Harlem area, which provided the detectives with yet another lead. Chief Quirk quickly contacted NYPD inspector Henry E. Buckman, who was the commanding officer of the Bronx detectives, and provided him with the details of the unidentified female and the discovery of the speakeasy cards found in the handbag near the body.[99] Yonkers detectives, assisted by NYPD detectives, armed with a photo of the dead woman,

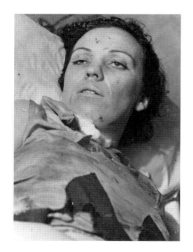

Virginia Brannen as she lay in the Stavey's Morgue on April 28, 1931. *Courtesy Yonkers PD.*

began their canvass of the speakeasies in the Harlem area based on the cards found in the handbag. Information obtained as a result of their speakeasy canvasses led them to the Primrose Dance Club.

By late the following night, Tuesday, April 28, the detectives had tentatively identified the dead woman as Virginia "Joyce" Brannen. A photo was shown to her best friend, Gertrude McDonald, but it wasn't until the next day that Gertrude made the positive identification after viewing Virginia's body at the Yonkers morgue. Police Chief Quirk then contacted the Bangor Maine Police via teletype to make the official notification to Virginia's family of her death.[100]

"Take Me to a Hospital"

The news of Virginia's mysterious death caused a stir throughout the Bangor area, and the Bangor police began to check over their reports for anything that might be helpful to the Yonkers police. One report, taken the previous month, stood out: on the night of March 12 around 11:00 p.m., Bangor PD patrolman Earl Heal, who was with patrol driver Levi Lambert, received a report that a car from New York was parked on Webster Avenue, a residential street in Bangor, and the occupants were acting suspiciously. Upon further investigation, the police found Virginia Brannen sitting inside the suspicious car with a man identified as Charles La Proto of 158 Newman Avenue, New York City. Virginia's friend Gertrude McDonald was in the front yard of a nearby house with an unidentified male who fled when the police approached them. As there appeared to be nothing criminal going on, the only police action taken was Patrolman Heal and Lambert drove Virginia home, while Gertrude and Charles La Porto drove off in the car. No further explanation was provided about what had transpired between the subjects or why the unidentified male fled. Patrolman Heal had made a written notation of the vehicle's New York plate number—6 U 801 at the time—and passed it along to the Yonkers detectives.[101]

Meanwhile, the Yonkers detectives were being assisted by NYPD inspector Harry E. Buckman and his dogged detectives Dominik Caso and William Mara out of the Forty-Second Squad in the Bronx. They began to focus their investigation on the Harlem speakeasies and dance clubs for any useful information after finding Virginia's missing brown shoe discarded on a main roadway that crossed the New York City border heading toward Yonkers. They believed that she may have been murdered in New York City.[102] Gertrude McDonald was unable to provide the detectives with any information about Virginia's activities or whereabouts for the past Sunday night, other than she was working at the Primrose until it closed; after that, she didn't know where Virginia went or with who. It was NYPD detectives Caso and Mara who receiving additional information from one of the other dancers at the Primrose Club that Virginia was seen getting into a late-model Chrysler sedan with Robert LeClair and Mildred Moore after the club closed on Sunday night.[103]

Sometime on Thursday afternoon, April 30, Detectives Caso and Mara picked up Robert and Mildred and brought them to the Morrisania Street (42nd) precinct for questioning. Robert refused to speak or cooperate with the police until he was informed that he and Mildred were the main subjects of their police investigation. That's when Robert said, "Send for a priest and we'll tell all." With that, Father Joseph McCafferty of the Church of the Resurrection at 131st Street and Broadway was summoned. Robert and Mildred then provided varying accounts, using the excuse that they were intoxicated and sleepy from three days of drinking and dancing and couldn't remember very much of the shooting. Robert LeClair was also acutely aware that Crowley didn't have any use for squealers, or rats, as he called them, and he would "take care" of anyone who ratted him out to the police. They were both held as material witnesses to Virginia's murder in the Yonkers Jail.[104] Subsequently, the NYPD recovered the murder car: the stolen Chrysler Imperial was riddled with police bullets and abandoned in front of 288 East 155th Street after four members of the Manhattan gun squad (current-day robbery squad) had exchanged shots with two male occupants in a running gun battle through the streets of the Bronx the night before.[105] Inside the stolen sedan, the detectives found a .22-caliber long gun in the backseat, along with four blankets, multiple spent rounds from a .38-caliber automatic hand gun and a large amount of dried blood on the backseat. Crowley had later bragged that he had shot it out with the cops using a machine gun.[106]

On Thursday April 30, 1931, Captain Harry Butts, NYPD's ballistic expert, reported that he had the opportunity to examine the bullets taken from the body of Detective Schaedel, who was shot by Crowley on March 13, and from the interior of the (gun squad) police car that had engaged in that wild gun battle, and the bullet that killed Virginia Brannen—it had been

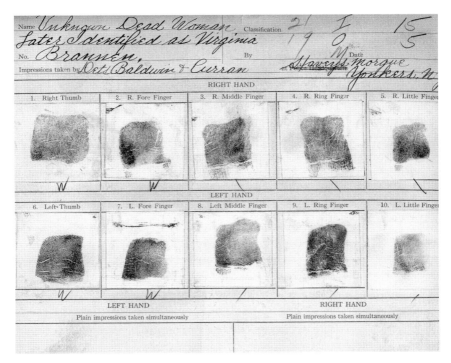

Fingerprints taken from Virginia Brannen's body by Yonkers detectives Baldwin and Curran in an effort to identify her. *Courtesy Yonkers PD.*

Bloodstained chalk outline of a bullet hole in the backseat cushion of the 1930 Chrysler Imperial sedan, showing where Duringer's bullet lodged after it passed through Virginia Brannen's chest, killing her. *Courtesy Yonkers PD.*

Outside view of the 1930 Chrysler Imperial sedan with bullet-riddled side rear window, results of Crowley's April 29 shootout with the NYPD. *Courtesy Yonkers PD.*

recovered from the rear seat of that Chrysler—and he found that all were fired from the same gun.[107] When this new information was made known to Robert LeClair, LeClair retracted his original statement and said that he had lied. Now he said that the man he described as Tommy Jordan was really Francis Crowley, and that Rudolph Duringer, who he named as the Virginia's killer, was, in fact, driving the stolen Chrysler when Virginia was shot. And it was Crowley who was sitting next to Virginia in the backseat and who had the pistol in his hand, not Duringer. LeClair maintained that he didn't actually see Crowley shoot Virginia, only that he heard a gunshot.

LeClair did, however, admit to being in the stolen sedan the night before and having a wild gun battle with the cops through the streets of the Bronx. It wasn't him shooting at the cops, it was Crowley; he maintained that he was only driving the car while Crowley was the one doing the actual shooting through the back window. The police quickly realized that they had two actual eyewitnesses to Virginia's murder, LeClair and Moore; however, there were creditability issues with both of their accounts of the murder. The big question was who actually fired that bullet into Virginia's chest, Crowley or Duringer?[108]

On Friday, May 1, 1931, Joseph Brannen, Virginia's father, arrived at the Harvey Funeral Home in Yonkers with Brannen family friend Alice Perro to

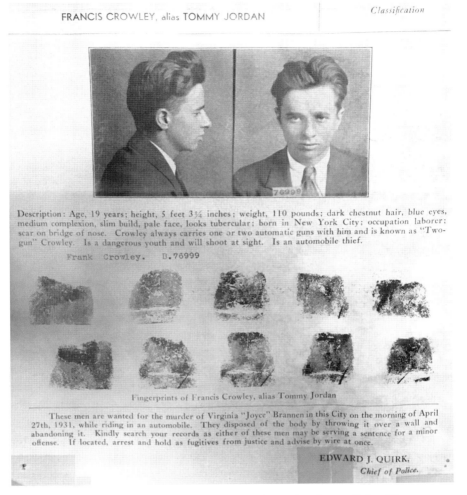

FRANCIS CROWLEY, alias TOMMY JORDAN

Classification

Description: Age, 19 years; height, 5 feet 3¼ inches; weight, 110 pounds; dark chestnut hair, blue eyes, medium complexion, slim build, pale face, looks tubercular; born in New York City; occupation laborer; scar on bridge of nose. Crowley always carries one or two automatic guns with him and is known as "Two-gun" Crowley. Is a dangerous youth and will shoot at sight. Is an automobile thief.

Frank Crowley. B.76999

Fingerprints of Francis Crowley, alias Tommy Jordan

These men are wanted for the murder of Virginia "Joyce" Brannen in this City on the morning of April 27th, 1931, while riding in an automobile. They disposed of the body by throwing it over a wall and abandoning it. Kindly search your records as either of these men may be serving a sentence for a minor offense. If located, arrest and hold as fugitives from justice and advise by wire at once.

EDWARD J. QUIRK,
Chief of Police.

Francis Crowley wanted poster for Virginia Brannen's murder. *Courtesy Yonkers PD.*

claim Virginia's body and to make the necessary arraignments to bring Virginia back home to Bangor. Joseph had taken the long, grieving journey by train the day before by himself, to shield Virginia's mother and her siblings from the heartache that lay ahead. When Joseph Brannen first viewed Virginia's body in the funeral home, he sorrowfully stated: "My poor child, I see she has dyed her lovely black curls red since leaving home. This city has killed her. Her mother and I thought she was working in a store here—we never knew she was in such a terrible business. This has broken her mother's heart."[109]

Rudolph Duringer wanted poster for Virginia Brannen's murder. *Courtesy Yonkers PD.*

Most, if not all, of Virginia's fellow dancers at the Primrose Club chipped in and donated a total of one hundred dollars in cash to give to the Brannen family so Virginia could be taken back to Bangor for a funeral and burial. Joseph Brannen left Yonkers on Friday, May 1, with his daughter's body for her final train ride home.[110]

On Monday June 1, 1931, Mildred Moore testified before Bronx supreme court justice Albert Cohn that she couldn't member all the events that occurred in the car on that fateful Monday morning. Though her testimony was short and fractured, it could be interpreted as somewhat of a self-serving remembrance. Mildred stated that she and Robert LeClair, whom she referred to as Bob, started out on Saturday afternoon, April 25, 1931, with Francis Crowley to go to Ossining to pick up Fats Duringer. She knew

Crowley and Duringer from the Primrose Dance Club, and her boyfriend Bob was friendly with them both. She said that she and Bob had emptied a couple of pints of gin on the way. Crowley was driving, and he wasn't drinking. When they picked up Fats, he bought some more pints and they drove back to New York. Then they drove out to Long Island because Francis wanted to say hello to his girlfriend out there. En route to Long Island, they bought some more pints of gin. When they returned to the city, they stopped at Mildred's apartment to clean up and they had some more drinks. Then they went to a speakeasy. Then they went to a restaurant, then another speakeasy, then to a dance hall, then another speakeasy. She couldn't provide any times, or locations, or names of the places they visited during their travels. The next day was Sunday, and she was so sleepy she didn't wake up in time to go to church. She further stated that she never misses church, ordinarily. They all slept at her apartment, getting up about noon, and then went to another speakeasy. Then they bought some more gin and went to visit a friend of hers at 220 West 114th Street. They drank the gin and left. Then they all went to a movie; she couldn't remember the name of the movie or what it was about. After that, they got two more pints of gin. By now, she stated, it was time to go to the Primrose Club, meaning to pick up Virginia Brannen after she had finished dancing for the night. The club usually opened at 8:00 p.m. and closed around 2:00 a.m. on the weekends. After they picked up Virginia and finally drove away, Mildred said that she was hungry for ham and eggs. She said she sat in the front seat of the car between Crowley and Bob LeClair. Mildred stated she was tired and sleepy and laid her head on Bob's shoulder. Virginia and Fats were in the backseat. Mildred also said that she would doze off occasionally, except when the car hit a bump. But, once it wasn't a bump: a gunshot from inside the car had awakened her, then a second gunshot. She looked around to the backseat. Virginia said, "Oh," and she was holding her right hand under her left breast. "Take me to a hospital," she cried. Bob said, "I guess she fainted," and Fats yelled to Bob, "Shut your mouth," and that's all Mildred heard, and that's all she said she remembered. District Attorney Charles B. McLaughlin questioned Mildred repeatedly about the circumstances of the shooting, but Mildred held to her story. The only thing she could add is that she and Bob had left the car before Duringer and Crowley tossed Virginia's body over that wall at Saint Joseph's Seminary in Yonkers.[111]

When Crowley learned that Mildred Moore and Robert LeClair had been picked up by the police earlier on Thursday, April 30, and were being held as witnesses in Virginia's murder, he and Billie Dunn quickly moved out of the 84th Street rooming house. They found a furnished fifth-floor walkup at 303 West 90th Street; this time, they used the last name of Dunn. Duringer couldn't go back to Ossining, so he bounced around the local pool halls until Crowley found the place on West 90th Street; then he stayed there, waiting for Crowley to come up with a plan.[112] Their West 90th Street hideout was on the top floor of an apartment building, with two small bedrooms and a galley kitchen that faced the back of the building. Billie and Crowley used one bedroom, while Duringer occupied the other.[113] Crowley didn't hang around; he didn't even spend the first night in the West 90th Street apartment. It wasn't in his personality to wait around; first thing he did was steal a car and head straight out to Long Island. For the next few days, Billie continued to dance at the Primrose Club at night, while Duringer just hung around the apartment eating and drinking or going to the neighborhood poolrooms.[114]

Long Island

Crowley would periodically visit Anna in Laurelton, though not so much to see her as much as to provide himself the opportunity to travel outside the of the city for potential crimes. He would venture father out past Laurelton into Nassau County. Crowley knew that one of Anna's Laurelton house borders, a guy named Aleck O'Neill, worked at a garden nursery in North Bellmore—not that Crowley had ever been friendly with him; he was just curious if he could benefit from it somehow.[115] However, Crowley had been friendly with a kid named Clinton Davis, who he used to play with back in the Bronx, when one or the other wasn't away in some children's home. Clinton was just a year younger than Crowley, and his family had recently moved out to a house on Montague Avenue at the corner of Clinton Avenue in North Merrick, Long Island.

The Davises had lived in an apartment building at 304 East 134th Street, just down from Anna and her baby mill. Clinton's father, Hugh Davis, was a house painter, and his mother, Edith Davis, had been hired as a retail clerk in a towel and haberdashery dry good store called The Beehive in Freeport, New York, the next village away from their home in North Merrick. Mr. and Mrs. Davis had two children, eighteen-year-old Clinton and nineteen-year-old daughter Eileen. But soon after the family moved to North Merrick, Eileen unfortunately came down with tuberculosis, requiring Edith to stay home to care for her. Her health continued to decline, and she succumbed to the disease in the fall of 1930.[116]

When Crowley did visit Clinton, it was usually away from the family residence, as Hugh and Edith didn't care for Crowley and his gangster-like behavior. In fact, Hugh Davis had cautioned Crowley sometime before Christmas 1930 to stay away from Clinton and their home.[117] At some point within the past year or so, Crowley had legally purchased an older Buick, though it was most likely purchased with proceeds from a robbery. Occasionally, he would bring it out to Clinton Davis if it needed some type of repair.[118] Clinton liked to work on cars, and he was good at making repairs—plus, he earned some much-needed money from the work. His friends and the locals who knew him called him "Tink," as he was always tinkering around with cars.[119] Through Tink, Crowley met some of the other local teenagers, such as Jonny Mc Cahill from Roosevelt, Salvatore Russo from Freeport and Howard Singer, who was also from Roosevelt, though a couple years younger than the rest of them.

Crowley's new Long Island acquaintances were easily impressed or maybe even fascinated by Crowley's continual bragging, bravado, rogue personality and seemingly prestigious New York City gangster lifestyle.[120] Stories of his robberies, the fast and exciting nightlife that he lived in the dance clubs and all those speakeasies he was so familiar with fascinated them. They had no reason to disbelieve his stories, even if he was smaller than most of them and sometimes struggled to pronounce certain words when he spoke of his exciting lifestyle. Plus, he always seemed to have plenty of cash and a fancy new car, and he always carried at least two, sometimes three, loaded handguns.[121] He would take them driving around the neighborhood and even buy them hot dogs from the local stand down on Sunrise Highway in Merrick. Crowley was completely different to them; it was like a living New York City crime legend coming right into their bucolic neighborhood, even if they had to be home before curfew. They would all later admit that they were always a little afraid of him, of what he might do, if provoked.[122]

Howard Singer was sixteen years old, and he lived on Allers Boulevard in Roosevelt with his mother, father, seven-year-old sister and six-month-old brother. Howard would later tell Nassau County police inspector Harold King in a sworn statement that he knew Crowley was doing stickups in Nassau County and that he knew he had robbed a dress store in the Merrick Gables. Singer also related that Crowley had fired a shot from one of his .38-caliber handguns one night into the wood floor of the candy store on Washington Avenue in Roosevelt. Singer also told Inspector King that he didn't actually see Crowley do the stickup or shoot into the floor, but all his friends knew he did the job, and the bullet was still lodged in the floor of the candy store.[123]

John Mc Cahill was nineteen years old, the same age as Crowley, and he boarded at 14 Bennett Avenue in Roosevelt. It's unknown what became of his parents, but his siblings were scattered throughout the area. His older brother Alex and older sister Beatrice boarded in separate homes in Roosevelt. Beatrice was dating a Hempstead Village cop, and a younger sister Evelyn, who was sixteen, lived at yet another address with a family named McKay at 165 Roosevelt Avenue, also in Roosevelt. John drove a local coal truck in the winter and an ice truck in the summer months.[124]

Salvatore Russo was also nineteen years old, and he lived at 28 North Main Street in Freeport with his mother, father, three sisters and one younger brother. Salvatore was known as "Solly" to his friends and worked with his father as a carpenter.[125]

Sometime in the summer of 1930, Crowley was doing his usual riding around the Roosevelt and Merrick area of Nassau County in one of his stolen cars trying to meet and impress the local kids with his bravado and tall tales, when one day he decided to go to a local south shore beach and met the pretty Helen Walsh. Helen was fifteen years old and lived in Brooklyn with her mother and older sister Margaret. Her mother and

Sixteen-year-old Helen Walsh.
Courtesy of the New York Daily News.

father were separated, so Helen would come out to Meader Avenue, in North Merrick, in the summer to spend time with her father, Jeremiah Walsh, then return to Brooklyn and spend the rest of the year with her mother, Margaret Walsh.[126] Her mother ran a boardinghouse at 190 Jay Street; she also had a second boardinghouse just around the corner at 69 Nassau Street in Brooklyn.[127]

As luck would have it, Helen and Crowley discovered that they both knew Johnny McCahill from Roosevelt. Crowley didn't know him that well; he only knew him through Tink Davis.[128] He was immediately taken by the young Helen's appearance and her proper behavior. Though she was four years younger than Crowley; intellectually, she was well beyond his nineteen years.

Still, Crowley was a street-smart and often underestimated adversary. Nevertheless, they appeared to share the same sophomoric spirit. Crowley's outlook was based on crime and all the dark elements associated with hate and violence toward anyone, mostly those who stood in his way of getting what he wanted.[129] Helen, on the other hand, seemed to be a little simpler, like any fifteen-year-old who struggles with the monumental problem of figuring where she fits into this world, perhaps even confused by her parent's relationship. It could be that she was just attracted to bad boys.[130] Whatever the reason, Crowley and Helen started spending more time together. Helen really didn't know Crowley or the life he led up in Harlem or the Bronx; he never took her there, and he didn't tell her either. After the summer ended and Helen returned to Brooklyn, he started spending time with Helen at her mother's house. But he didn't stop, or he couldn't stop, returning to the Bronx and the Primrose Club, or to Billie Dunn and his favorite pastime, stickups.[131]

To Helen's mother and father, Crowley seemed like a decent, though impulsive youth deeply in love with their daughter, and very anxious to marry her. Helen's mother was a stout, gray-haired older woman who would later confide to a reporter from the *New York Herald* that Crowley, who they called "Shorty,"

> *had always been polite to her, and appeared to be a nice chap. She said he earned $50.00 a week as a lather, and once before Christmas of last year when he came calling for Helen, and Helen wasn't home, he was so kind, he took me shopping in his new car. She said he was a good worker, kept himself neat and clean and owned his own car. She said she liked him very much.*[132]

Around the same time, just before Christmas 1930, Crowley asked Helen to marry him. Helen would later admit that when she first met Crowley, she liked him, but he soon became controlling and very, very jealous of her, even angry at her whenever she looked at someone else. For whatever reason, Helen accepted his offer of marriage, and Crowley gave Helen a $500 engagement ring. The engagement was short-lived; one night, while they were driving around in one of his stolen cars, they began to quarrel over his lifestyle and the company he kept in the Bronx, and Helen wanted him to stop hanging around with "those" people. Crowley refused, and Helen took the engagement ring off her finger and handed it back to him. Crowley got angry at her and threw the ring out of the car window. Helen's mother laughed it off, saying they made up a couple days later. Her mother also said that Helen always insisted that she didn't care as much for Crowley as he did for her. Helen's mother thought that Crowley's mind had been turned by his great love for her beautiful daughter and that he must have been led astray by others, though she didn't know who any of those others were.[133]

Helen was, for the most part, a bright, articulate and intelligent young girl. She attended Saint Vincent's Academy in Newark, New Jersey, from when she was seven years old until she was eleven; then she attended Saint James Parochial School in Brooklyn, graduating when she was fifteen. Helen wanted to venture out in the world and look for a job after finishing school, but her mother wouldn't have it; she wanted Helen to be an interior decorator, but that could come later. Margaret Walsh had saved up some money from her boardinghouses and insisted that Helen take the money and go buy some clothes and have a good time. Then, in time, if Helen wanted, she could study interior design.[134]

On Tuesday, May 5, 1931, at about 11:45 p.m. on a mild and windless spring night, Nassau County patrolman Fred S. Hirsch Jr., shield no. 207, was in Booth E, located on Nassau Road in the village of Roosevelt. Patrolman Hirsch was just completing his 4:00 p.m. to midnight tour of duty and was preparing to end his shift. He finished up the necessary paperwork that was required at the end of each tour, documenting all the police activity that occurred under his watch and waiting to be officially relieved by the next patrolman who would be covering the village booth foot post from midnight to 8:00 a.m.[135] Departmental rules and regulations stated that all police posts were to be face-to-face reliefs, with a starting time of ten minutes prior to the beginning of each tour, allowing for the oncoming patrolman to be briefed of any prior incidents or events that would be relevant to him or something that needed to be passed along to other officers. This night was no different; at 11:50 p.m. Patrolman Peter Yodice, shield no. 916, arrived at Booth E to relieve patrolman Hirsch.[136]

NCPD photo of Patrolman Fred S. Hirsch Jr., shield no. 207. *Courtesy NCPD museum.*

Fred (Ferdinand) S. Hirsch Jr. was born on April 10, 1900, in the Bronx to Ferdinand and Louise Hirsch of 804

Melrose Avenue. Fred was the son of French and German immigrants and the product of a loving family. His father managed his own butcher shop, while his mother maintained the home and raised him, an older sister and one younger brother. After completing his education in the Bronx, Fred worked as an electrician for a contractor in the New York City area. On September 15, 1921, Fred married Freda Schultz, who was also from the Bronx. They lived in the Bronx until just after the birth of their first child, Felicia, in 1922; then they relocated to the suburbs in Nassau County, to a private house at 305 Hicks Street in Bellmore. There Fred and Freda would have two additional children: Cecelia, who was born in 1925, and Ferdinand (Wallace), who was born in 1927.[137] Both Fred and his wife were devout Roman Catholics, and they lived within walking distance to Saint Barnabas's Church and School, which their children would later attend. Fred was a devoted husband, and an adoring and loving father. He was also ardent about providing the best and safest environment for his young and growing family and his community. Fred was described as a kind and caring Christian to all those who would come to know him, whether they were his Bellmore neighbors, coworkers or the people on his police beat.[138]

8

The Black Shirts

The Nassau County Police Department was established on April 16, 1925, with fifty-five handpicked men from the Nassau County Sheriff's Department. The county was relatively young, created only twenty-six years before the police department, in 1899. It was born out of the political abandonment of New York City's Queens County, when Queens joined the other four boroughs of New York and became part of Greater New York. For whatever reason, the powers that be refused to include the three eastern towns of Queens into their new Greater New York: the Town of Hempstead, the Town of North Hempstead and the Town of Oyster Bay, which bordered Suffolk County to the east. So, the three abandoned and dejected towns got together and petitioned New York State to become their own county. Though these communities would have preferred to enjoy the economic benefits of being included in the Greater New York region, in 1899, the state approved their petition. The population of Nassau County rapidly increased from its beginning in 1899 from around 50,000 to over 300,000 by 1925, due in part to the increased use of a reliable railroad service into New York City and the growing use of private automobiles. As people began moving east toward safety and security in the pastoral countryside of Nassau County and away from the hectic and crime-ridden frenzy of New York City, they unwittingly brought with them an increase in crime, causing great concern to the residents of Nassau County and necessitating the creation of a police department.[139]

Nassau County Police recruit class, April 4, 1928. Patrolman Fred S. Hirsch Jr. is on the first row, second from the right. *Courtesy NCPD museum.*

With the county's 287 square miles of land and 166 miles of Atlantic Ocean and Long Island Sound shoreline, its population continued to expand.[140] By 1928, the Nassau County Police Department had also witnessed a measured increase, from its original 55 patrolmen, to the appointment of its 295th patrolman, Fred S. Hirsch Jr., one in a recruit class of 25 appointed on April 4, 1928.[141] At five feet, nine inches, the brown-haired, blue-eyed, soft-spoken and diligent recruit was assigned to the First Precinct in Merrick, which covered a large slice of the county's southern villages.[142] Within a year and a half after Fred's appointment to the Nassau County Police Department, the couple had their fourth and last child, a son they named John Warren Hirsch.[143] Fred remained in the First Precinct, except for a short stint when he was reassigned to the newly formed Fourth Precinct; after six months, he returned to the First Precinct.[144]

Hirsch lived and worked on a simple principle. He was committed to fairness for all, whether he was working as a cop or in the community he was raising his family in, which wasn't an opinion shared by all. Hirsch and his family resided in Bellmore, which fell within the confines of his command, the First Precinct. On January 6, 1931, he was chastised by his commanding officer, Acting Captain Gordon E. Hurley, for signing a petition in favor of a Catherine Van Singer, also a resident of Bellmore, maintaining a junkyard in a sparsely populated area. The petition was being generated to change the Town of Hempstead's building and zoning ordinance. The captain charged that Hirsch had no right to sign the petition when Joseph Parsons, the chief building inspector for the Town of Hempstead, had already issued Catherine Van Singer a summons for operating a junkyard on her property in violation of the town's ordinance. Hirsch explained to the Captain that he had signed Van Singer's petition well before Parsons had ever issued her the summons. Hirsch was then ordered by the captain to respond to Parsons's office forthwith and remove his name from that petition—and in the future refrain from putting his signature on anything contrary to a law.[145]

Peter J. Yodice was born on September 28, 1898, in Naples, Italy, the only child of Bernardo and Rosina Yodice, who immigrated to the United States in 1901. Peter's family settled in Farmingdale, New York, where his father established a construction business making cement sewer pipes. Peter married Josephine Desantis when he was about twenty-five years old, and together they had four children. Though Peter's education didn't go beyond the sixth grade, he spent almost twenty years laboring in his father's cement business until the Great Depression and the collapse of the construction business forced him to another career.[146] On January 1, 1931, Peter Yodice was appointed to the Nassau County Police Department and assigned to the First Precinct, bringing the strength of the department up to around five hundred.[147]

Patrolman Yodice would later on the morning of May 6, 1931, give his sworn statement of events that led to the murder of Patrolman Hirsch to Nassau County assistant district attorney Albert M. DeMeo at police headquarters in Mineola, New York. In that statement, Yodice stated that after he pulled up to the police booth, he was removing his equipment from his car when he was approached by a local taxicab driver by the name of A.E. Fowler. Fowler told Yodice that a few minutes earlier he had picked up a passenger named Ramsbottom and drove him east into the village of Merrick by way of Washington Avenue, where he passed three men walking west; at the time, they didn't have anything in their hands. Then, about fifteen minutes later, when he was

NCPD photo of Patrolman Peter Yodice, shield number 916, serial number 392. *Courtesy NCPD museum.*

returning to Roosevelt, Fowler saw the same three men at Astor Place and Washington Avenue heading east, carrying some car tires. Fowler stated that it was too dark for him to see if he knew them or not, but he knew they were the same ones he passed earlier. Fowler further stated that he thought they might have stolen the tires from the Roosevelt School on Washington Avenue. Yodice then proceeded into the police booth and telephoned the First Precinct desk officer, Lieutenant Baumann. He also officially signed on duty and proceeded to tell Lieutenant Baumann what he had been told by the taxicab driver.[148]

In 1931, each precinct had a tour-of-duty desk officer, usually a lieutenant, who delegated any and all police-related assignments during that tour and who was ultimately responsible for everything that occurred in his precinct during that tour. In police jargon, the lieutenant was "on the hook" for everything that either happened or didn't happen during his tour in his precinct.[149] As Yodice was talking with the desk officer, Hirsch finished his paperwork and listened to Yodice's telephone conversation.[150] Most, if not all Nassau County police booths in 1931 had only one chair and a small desk and could not accommodate more than three or four police officers at any one time, provided that they were all standing up.[151] Yodice hung up the phone, made no comment to Hirsch and excitedly rushed out the door to his private car. Hirsch stopped him and said, "Wait a minute, where are you going?" Yodice told Hirsch that the desk officer authorized him to go investigate this possible stolen tire report. It remains unclear why Lieutenant Bauman authorized Yodice, a rookie cop, to take his own private car away from his assigned foot post to investigate the possible theft of stolen tires in an unfamiliar area, especially with such limited information. The lieutenant could have just as easily taken the information from Yodice and passed it along to the motor patrol car assigned to that area to investigate.[152]

In 1931, Nassau police vehicles didn't have radio communication with their command; that technology wouldn't be available until around 1933.[153] So, it could be that the desk officer realized that time was of the essence to recover the tires and apprehend the three perpetrators, as there had been an increasing number of car tire thefts in the area. Hirsch realized that Yodice was excited about the desk officer authorizing him, a rookie, to conduct this investigation. Though he knew he was a couple years older than him, Hirsch also knew Yodice had been a cop for only four months, and any number of things could happen to an inexperienced cop, overexcited, outnumbered and alone. For the most part, Yodice was behaving like an excitable rookie, which is not uncommon at times, even today. Inasmuch as Hirsch wanted to go home for the night, he told Yodice, "Wait, I'll go with you." The newer officer accepted his offer for help with an OK. Less than ten to twelve minutes had lapsed since taxicab driver Fowler informed Yodice of the possible theft. Both patrolmen got into Yodice's Plymouth sedan and headed east on Washington Avenue; they passed the school mentioned by the witness and continued east toward Meadowbrook. They saw three youths walking in the roadway on the north side of Washington just west of the Meadowbrook Creek bridge, about three hundred feet west of Meadowbrook Road. Later that Wednesday morning, as Patrolman Yodice continued with his sworn statement to ADA Albert M. DeMeo, the attorney had to interrupt the excitable patrolman and remind him to stay calm, not to talk so fast and try to be a little more distinct. Before the completion of his short-sworn statement, ADA DeMeo had to remind Yodice three additional times to stay calm, talk slower and take his time as he revisited the events that unfolded.[154]

Meanwhile, Johnny McCahill, Tink and Solly had left the poolroom on Nassau Road in Roosevelt sometime before midnight and were walking east on Washington Avenue toward Meadowbrook Road, which was close to Tink's house. According to John McCahill's sworn statement to ADA DeMeo at police headquarters later in the day on Wednesday May 6, Tuesday, the day before, he and Tink had driven out toward Jones Beach to the new causeway under construction. Even though McCahill already had a job, the two drove out to see if they could get truck driving jobs. They were told the road crew wasn't hiring, so they drove back to Helen Walsh's house in North Merrick. Johnny said he and Tink picked her up to go riding around in his old Chrysler roadster. They decided to park down by the Meadowbrook Creek bridge on Washington Avenue, where they just talked, the three of them. That's when Helen told McCahill and Tink that the fellows in the city didn't have blackheads on their faces, that he and Tink were just a couple country hicks and didn't know anything. So, Johnny said he and Tink let Helen squeeze the blackheads out of their faces while they sat in the car by the bridge. Johnny said a little while later they saw this new Ford come flying up on them; Shorty stuck his hand out of the car window and waved to them. Then Shorty turned around and came back to where they were, and he said to Tink, "Let's go over to your house."

Tink later said he was scared to refuse, so they all went over to Tink's house on Clinton Avenue, which was only two blocks east of Meadowbrook Road and real close to Black Shirt Lane in North Merrick. Then Shorty wanted Tink to show him where Aleck O'Neill, who boarded with Shorty's mother in Laurelton, worked. Tink agreed, and the rest of them drove to the

Sunrise Nursery at Jerusalem and Park Avenues in North Bellmore. Crowley was always scouting for an easy stickup location—many times, these were associated with people he knew. It was a lot easier than casing a new and unfamiliar location; plus, he was lazy. Then they rode around for a while longer. They drove back and forth along the Southern State Parkway and on Sunrise Highway for a while. After a while, they picked up Solly in Freeport and drove over to Washington Avenue and parked on the dirt lane about three hundred feet west from Meadowbrook Road.

McCahill called it Black Shirt Lane because that was the name of their gang. It was a loosely composed group consisting of John McCahill, Clinton Davis, Howard Singer and a few other trusted neighborhood kids who may have still belonged to the Black Shirts or moved on as they matured. A couple years earlier, they had built a hut back up in the woods, at the far end of the lane. All the local kids referred to the narrow dirt road as Black Shirt Lane, but the Town of Hempstead's official name for it was Morris Avenue. Morris Avenue was narrow, with barely just enough room for one car to pass through the 15-to-20-foot-tall thickets and late growth of trees that lined both sides. The dirt lane wasn't any longer than 500 or 600 feet, with a convenient circular turnaround cut out of the thickets at the far end to accommodate one vehicle. Morris Avenue ran south off Washington Avenue about 300 feet west from the T-intersection where Washington Avenue met Meadowbrook Road in North Merrick. There was only one residence, a small summer cottage, located on the west side of the lane just about 150 feet off Washington Avenue. It was rarely used and almost completely obstructed from view by the dense thickets and trees along the dirt lane. The property belonged to a G.R. Langer of 175 East 82nd Street, New York City, according to the hand-painted sign nailed to a tree in front of the now vacant summer bungalow.[155]

Washington Avenue was a flat, straight, concrete road, only 1.3 miles from the police booth on Nassau Road to the end, where it met Meadowbrook Road. The single-family wood frame houses on Washington Avenue were few and far between. As Yodice and Hirsch drove east on Washington looking for the three tire thieves, they came across McCahill, Solly and Tink walking near the Meadowbrook Creek bridge.[156] Yodice and Hirsch stopped their car, got out and approached them. Hirsch recognized McCahill. A few months earlier, McCahill approached Hirsch and asked him to "flash" a ticket for him, a term that meant dismissing the charge. Hirsch asked McCahill what the ticket was for, and McCahill told him, "I passed a car on the right." Hirsch said OK, and McCahill gave him the

Washington Avenue looking west from Meadowbrook Road, North Merrick. Morris Avenue (Black Shirt Lane) is the first left after the first telephone pole on the left, just before the Meadowbrook Creek bridge. Crime scene photo taken early morning on Wednesday May 6, 1931. *Courtesy NCPD.*

ticket, then thanked him. McCahill would later state that when he asked Hirsch how much money he wanted for fixing the ticket, Hirsch said he didn't want money, it was a favor.[157] What Hirsch and Yodice didn't know when they stopped the three was that earlier, when McCahill, Tink and Solly had walked up to the poolroom on Nassau Road, they had just left Crowley and Helen Walsh, who were parked on Black Shirt Lane not two hundred feet from where they now stood.

They all had been riding around together in Crowley's stolen Ford, when Crowley parked up in the back of Black Shirt Lane and told McCahill, Tink and Solly to get out of the car so he could be alone with Helen. They took one of Crowley's other guns, a .38-caliber silver Smith & Wesson five-shot revolver from a bag on the front seat of the Ford. Crowley had also given them an extra five rounds to shoot off in the woods. Solly was carrying the gun, but he decided to hide it under the Meadowbrook Creek bridge in his hat while they went up to the poolroom. Solly had just retrieved the gun from under the bridge when they were stopped by Hirsch and Yodice. When Yodice and Hirsch exited their car, McCahill, Tink and Solly were surprised when they realized that the two were uniformed cops. Out of view from the car's headlights, and unbeknownst to Yodice and Hirsch, Solly casually tossed the silver-colored revolver into the grass on the side of the road. While Hirsch was talking with McCahill and Yodice was distracted talking with Solly, Tink coolly removed the five extra bullets from his pants pocket and threw them into the dark grass behind him. For whatever reason, Yodice and Hirsch didn't separate or question the three any longer, nor did they physically search them. This was perhaps because Hirsch was familiar with McCahill or they were both satisfied that the three weren't the tire thieves they were looking for. So, when Tink said they were heading to his house a couple blocks away, Yodice and Hirsch let them go.[158]

Silver-colored five-shot, Smith & Wesson revolver discarded by Salvatore "Solly" Russo and five live bullets discarded by Clinton "Tink" Davis when approached by Patrolmen Yodice and Hirsch by the Meadowbrook Creek bridge. Bullets sit atop the metal cans for crime scene photo purposes. *Courtesy NCPD.*

Just as Yodice and Hirsch were getting back into their car, Patrolman Kreutziger, also from the First Precinct, and just on duty to operate the motor patrol vehicle for that area, pulled up to them and asked what was going on. After he was informed by Hirsch of the details of their investigation, he stated that he just came up Meadowbrook Road and didn't see anyone other than the three guys they had just released. Patrolman Kreutziger said that he would go and patrol the streets south of Washington Avenue and keep a look out for the tire thieves, then drove away. As Yodice and Hirsch pulled back out onto Washington Avenue from the north side of the road and headed east, their headlights flashed across a darkened parked car set back off the road on Morris Avenue. When they got to Meadowbrook Road, they made a quick U-turn and headed back west on Washington for about three hundred feet and made a fast, hard left onto Morris Avenue, stopping just off Washington. With their headlights illuminating the front of the late-model Ford, they could see two occupants in the sedan, which was parked about sixty feet deep onto Morris facing out toward Washington. The patrolmen exited their car and approached the Ford on foot.[159]

9

"It Sounded Like a Machine Gun"

Earlier, when Crowley kicked McCahill, Solly and Tink out of the car so he could be alone with Helen, they had been parked back in the circular turnaround at the end of Morris Avenue, but he felt uncomfortable, even a little paranoid, so he moved the car closer to Washington Avenue in case he needed to make a quick getaway. Crowley didn't trust anyone, and he wanted to be prepared for anything. He had no sooner moved the car closer to Washington Avenue than Yodice and Hirsch suddenly pulled onto Morris with their headlights beaming directly into his car. Helen was still in the backseat, but Crowley had positioned the car in such a manner that if anyone did approach him, it would have to be from the passenger side door. He left no room between the driver's side door and the thick underbrush at the lane's edge.[160] With the sudden appearance of Yodice's car and its glaring headlights, Crowley was startled, and he quickly turned the Ford's headlights on. With both vehicles' headlights illuminating the short distance between the two vehicles, both Yodice and Hirsch could clearly be seen and identified as the police in uniform. Their double-breasted dark blue regulation coats bore ten brass buttons in double lines of five down the front, and their hats had a large metal shield at the peak. Both patrolmen's coats had a large metal police shield on the left breast.[161]

Both Yodice and Hirsch approached Crowley's vehicle together. Hirsch was walking ahead of Yodice, and he opened the front passenger door. As they both leaned into the vehicle, Yodice shone his flashlight into the front seat, while Hirsch turned his flashlight to the backseat of the vehicle and asked Helen her name and age. Helen said her name was Mary McCahill and she was seventeen years old. When asked by Hirsch if her mother knew she was out this late, she stated, "Yes." Yodice testified that when he told the driver to remove his hat, the driver said, "Why certainly, officer." He took his hat off and acted very friendly, just like a little kid would, Yodice added. The patrolman said he couldn't see a scar, that he put the flashlight right on the driver's face, but he couldn't see a scar. He told him to put his hat back on, and he did. Yodice would later testify that he thought the driver resembled Crowley from the wanted poster that was hung up in the police booth, but he didn't see the scar on the bridge of his nose.

Meanwhile, Hirsch was looking at Helen, and he seemed puzzled. It was later revealed in court testimony that Hirsch knew the McCahills; in fact, he had just let Johnny McCahill walk away on Washington Avenue, which would have been within sight of this car had it been daylight. He knew Johnny's sister Beatrice Mc Cahill was dating a Hempstead Village cop named Matthews, and they had another younger sister named Evelyn. But he had never heard or seen a Mary McCahill before tonight. Hirsch became suspicious. Yodice testified that Hirsch seemed interested in the girl, that he thought that maybe Hirsch knew her from somewhere. He said to Hirsch, "Come on, there is nothing to this," and Hirsch replied, "No, wait a minute, we might as well check up on the license." Hirsch, still standing between the open door and the body of the car, then asked Crowley for his driver's license. Yodice turned and walked back toward the front of the car, standing aside, with his back to Hirsch. All of a sudden, he heard multiple gunshots fired in a rapid succession from inside the car. Yodice turned to face the car but looked into the glaring bright lights of the Ford's headlights, which obscured his vision.

It was later determined that both of Crowley's automatic pistols were fully loaded; each magazine held seven bullets with another bullet in each chamber. Crowley had savagely fired a total of sixteen shots; the last two threw the right front corner of the car's windshield at Yodice. The deafening gunshots and bright flashes coming from the interior of the car startled Yodice, throwing him off balance, and he staggered backward across the dirt lane and fell into the bushes as he struggled to remove his service weapon from his holster, trapped beneath his heavy overcoat. As Yodice managed to scramble to his feet, he was able to remove his service revolver. Without aiming, and in a disordered state, he fired all six shots at the Ford—not twenty feet away—and missed every one. But before he could reload, the Ford started and jerked its way out of the lane, passing around Yodice's car at a rapid pace. Then it turned left onto Washington Avenue and disappeared in the dark. Yodice said he continued to awkwardly stumble through the dense thickets parallel with Morris Avenue until he reached Washington Avenue, just in time to see Crowley's car fade from view. Yodice would also testify that when the shooting started, he thought to himself that he had them, that he had their car blocked in and that they couldn't get away, that they couldn't get past his car. He couldn't see Hirsch, but he heard him holler out three times "OH! OH! OH!" And by the *bing, bing, bing* sounds of the gunshots whizzing around the car, they must have been shooting from two or three guns. "It sounded like a machine gun," Yodice would later say. He also stated that Crowley was shooting like the devil.[162]

After Yodice finally stumbled out of the woods to the concrete roadway of Washington Avenue, he was near exhaustion. With the thumping of his heartbeat deep within his ears, he ran back to Morris Avenue to find Hirsch. During the shooting, and in his excited state as he raced for cover, he had dropped his flashlight in the dirt by the front of the Ford. He picked up the light, only to see Hirsch lying on his back at the edge of

Two Gun Crowley's stolen 1930 maroon Ford sedan as it was positioned on Black Shirt Lane when approached by Yodice and Hirsch. Re-created by investigating Nassau detectives on May 10, 1931. *Courtesy NCPD.*

the dirt lane, parallel to where the Ford was parked. The top of Hirsch's head was pointed in the direction of Washington Avenue. Yodice shook Hirsch by the front of his coat and repeatedly called his name for any sign of life. The night's temperature was just forty degrees, but Yodice was sweating profusely as he knelt in the dirt alongside Hirsch and shone his flashlight into Hirsch's stark, ashen face. He realized Hirsch was dead. In the eerie stillness, Yodice ran back to his car, started it up and threw the car into reverse. With the pedal pressed to the floor, the rear wheels spun and whined for traction, throwing dirt and rocks in the air before they suddenly gripped the solid concrete of Washington Avenue. All the while, by touch, Yodice was trying to reload the open cylinder of his service revolver, which was wedged between his inner thighs, barrel down. The loose bullets fell from his shaking, sweat-covered fingers. He raced the 1.3 miles west on the blackened and deserted roadway to Booth E to call Lieutenant Baumann, to tell him that Hirsch had been shot and was presumably dead. Yodice gave the desk officer the location of the shooting. At 12:25 a.m., Patrolman Kreutziger, the midnight motor patrol operator, pulled up to the booth as Yodice was hanging up. Yodice quickly

Patrolman Yodice's personal Plymouth sedan as he had it positioned when they approached Two Gun Crowley's Ford on Black Shirt Lane. *Courtesy NCPD.*

The body of Patrolman Fred S. Hirsch Jr. His hat rests on the side of the dirt lane in the foreground from his body, an indication as to the violent effects of fourteen bullets fired into his body at close range. *Courtesy NCPD.*

updated the senior patrolman about what had happened. Kreutziger then told Yodice to take Patrolman Drake, who was with Kreutziger, back to the scene and that he would get Dr. Parsons, who lived just down the block on Nassau Road near Debevois Avenue.[163]

At 12:35 a.m., Detective Bert Bedell, with Detective Sergeant Vaughan and Detective Brinsley from the First Precinct Detective Squad out of the Freeport Police Department Headquarters, were the first detectives to arrive on scene.[164] A short time before them, Patrolmen Yodice and Drake arrived back at the scene, and a few local people began to gather at the entrance to Morris Avenue. That's when Patrolman Drake overheard McCahill say out loud, "Gee, its Art Hirsch," and he grabbed McCahill, telling one of the detectives that this guy knew Hirsch. McCahill was taken over to a police car parked on the shoulder of Washington Avenue near the entrance to Morris Avenue to be interviewed. Patrolman Yodice identified McCahill as one of the guys he and Hirsch had let go a few minutes before the shooting and noted that he had the same last name as the girl who was in the backseat of the car. McCahill was initially uncooperative, but he eventually told the detectives that she wasn't a McCahill, that her real name was Helen Walsh, and the driver of the car was Francis Crowley.[165] McCahill stopped short of revealing anything more and lied to the detectives when he said that Russo wasn't in Crowley's car with him and Tink earlier. He told the detectives that he and Tink met up with Solly at the poolroom after they had already left Walsh and Crowley on Black Shirt Lane. He also denied any knowledge of stolen car tires. Tink was also interviewed at the scene by the detectives. His recollection of movements prior to the shooting were also vague and misleading. Edith Davis was questioned at the scene as well, but she was belligerent and became abusive toward the detectives, refusing to answer any of their questions. She even went so far as to say, "I wish you detectives would just break your necks." When she was cautioned by a detective about her tone and her threats, she ignored the warning and went on to say that some New York City detectives had come by her house a few days before and accused her of running a whorehouse and harboring the gangster Francis Crowley. In Russo's initial interview at the scene, he stated that he didn't know anything about the car or its occupants, or any stolen tires, and that he had just met up with McCahill and Tink at the poolroom earlier. Inspector King then ordered McCahill, Clinton "Tink" Davis and his mother, Edith Davis, to be arrested as material witnesses and transported to police headquarters in Mineola for further questioning. Salvatore "Solly" Russo was released and free to go.[166]

Johnny McCahill would later tell Inspector King and ADA Albert DeMeo at Nassau County Police Headquarters in Mineola that the cops "nailed them on Washington Avenue, because somebody must have grabbed some tires, or something." They let them go off to Tink's house. McCahill continued:

> So Tink, he just gets in the door and puts on the radio, and we were just in the doorway, just closing the door when the shots go off, you know, with the door half open and half closed. I was scared more than anything because I am no use around a gun. So, we goes out, and we goes back there.[167]

McCahill gave a deceptive and moronic recollection of the events, stating that he, Tink, Solly and Mrs. Davis all walked back down to Black Shirt Lane, and when they get there, a blond cop he had seen around Roosevelt told them to get out of there: "Don't hang around here." They couldn't get a good look down Black Shirt Lane from where they were standing on Washington, so they all went back to Tink's house. About twenty minutes later, they all decided to return to see what was going on, even Mrs. Davis. McCahill got closer this time and saw Hirsch's body lying there, exclaiming, "Gee, it's Art Hirsch." Why McCahill called Hirsch "Art" was never made clear.[168]

By 12:50 a.m., Chief of Detectives Harold King and Captain Morse had also arrived at the scene. They were followed by District Attorney Elvin Edwards and his team of assistant district attorneys: Brown, DeMeo, Spoor and Littleton. Once at the scene, King gave the order for all Nassau County detectives, on or off duty, to immediately respond to the scene. The crime scene quickly became an outdoor command post to disseminate known information and a gathering place for the detectives to share theories on how and where to draw out and apprehend this killer, all the while Patrolman Hirsch's body lay motionless on the cold dirt lane.[169]

At 12:48 a.m., Dr. Rudolph Parsons of 231 Nassau Road was brought to the scene by Patrolman Kreutziger and pronounced Patrolman Hirsch dead of multiple gunshot wounds.

Just some of the Nassau County detectives assigned to investigate Patrolman Fred S. Hirsch Jr.'s murder. Chief of Detectives Harold King is fifth from the right. *Courtesy NCPD museum.*

At about 1:10 a.m. Detectives Bedell and Bachman, along with Detective Sergeant Vaughan, took Patrolman Yodice to 14 Bennett Avenue in Roosevelt, the home of Mr. and Mrs. Joseph McClure, where John McCahill was a boarder. They were looking for the girl from the backseat of Crowley's car, as only Patrolman Yodice could make a positive identification. The McClures told the detectives and Yodice that no girl by Yodice's description lived at that house. However, they did identify the wanted poster with the photo of Francis Crowley that they were shown by the detectives as someone they knew only as "Shorty." He had come looking for Johnny McCahill there a couple of times in the past. The

Nassau County police chief of detectives, Inspector Harold King, led the investigation into the murder of Patrolman Fred S. Hirsch Jr. *Courtesy NCPD museum.*

detectives then went to the home of McCahill's sister Beatrice Mc Cahill at 448 Nassau Road, and they learned that she had not left the house since her boyfriend, Hempstead Village patrolman Wesley Matthews, shield no. 27, had departed earlier, at 11:30 p.m.[170]

10

The Dragnet

Back at Black Shirt Lane, at around 2:05 a.m., Detectives Closs and McCauley overheard a conversation between a man and woman at the scene discussing the gunshots they heard earlier. They were identified as a husband and wife—Robert Cooper, twenty-three, and Ruth Cooper, twenty-one—who resided on Bridge Street off Meadowbrook Road in North Merrick, just around the corner from Black Shirt Lane by road, but a shorter distance through the woods. They stated that at about 12:25 a.m., they heard at least twelve gunshots in rapid succession coming from the Black Shirt Lane area. Ruth Cooper also stated that after she heard the shots, she heard the roar of a car motor and then the sound of a police whistle blowing four times. Black Shirt Lane quickly became a swarm of police activity and gathered its share of onlookers as well. Yodice would later testify that he didn't remember blowing his police whistle.[171]

At 3:10 a.m., acting county coroner Wilbur Southard arrived at the scene and was quickly assisted by detectives to conduct a further examination of Patrolman Hirsch's body. They found multiple gunshot wounds to his chest, with either another gunshot wound or exiting bullet wound striking his right wrist. It hit his wristwatch and sent the pieces to the ground near his feet. The examination also revealed that Hirsch's service revolver was missing from the holster. With the completion of photos of the body and the scene, Patrolman Hirsch's body was removed to Southard's coroner morgue in Wantagh, New York, accompanied by Inspector King and Detectives Shanley and Hizinski, where they took possession of Hirsch's bullet-riddled police uniform for evidence.[172]

Investigating detectives examine Patrolman Hirsch's dead body for evidence. *Courtesy NCPD museum.*

At 3:20 a.m., detectives responded to the home of Merle McKay at 165 Roosevelt Avenue, where they learned McCahill's younger sister Evelyn lived. Evelyn was sixteen years old, and her whereabouts at the time of the shooting of Patrolman Hirsch were accounted for by the homeowner, who stated that Evelyn had been in bed with her at that time and hadn't left her side since. A thorough ground search of the scene and surrounding area was conducted by every patrolman and detective; they were searching for Patrolman Hirsch's missing service revolver. It was at this time that homicide detective Culkin came across a loaded silver Smith & Wesson revolver, serial no. 98521, and five live bullets in the grass on Washington Avenue, where Russo and Tink had thrown them earlier.[173]

At 3:32 a.m., Detective McCauley notified the teletype bureau in police headquarters via telephone to add an addendum to Nassau alarm no. 726, which had been broadcasted earlier to nationwide police departments to be on the lookout for Francis "Two Gun" Crowley. The addendum was added for Patrolman Hirsch's service revolver, a Smith & Wesson .38-caliber six-shot revolver, serial no. 583898, stolen during the commission of his murder.[174]

Sometime after Patrolman Hirsch's body was removed by the county coroner, a small delegation of high-ranking uniformed officers and detectives, accompanied by the departmental chaplain, responded to Patrolman

Hirsch's home in Bellmore to inform his wife, Freda, and his four children that her husband and their father had been murdered.[175]

At 8:45 a.m., Nassau County Police were notified by NYPD's Captain Graham that two of his men from the 103rd Detective Squad had recovered an abandoned maroon 1930 Ford sedan at the Long Island Rail Road train station on New York Avenue in Jamaica, New York, with plate no. 2C-64-39 and motor number 3754804. Five spent .38 ACP (automatic Colt pistol) cartridges were found on the front seat, with another five spent rounds of the same caliber found on the rear seat of the vehicle. The vehicle had a partially broken out windshield on the right (passenger) side, and it was registered to Henry Bernestein of 232 East 6th Street, Manhattan. The car was reported stolen the day before, May 5, 1931, and NYPD stolen car alarm no. 12461 broadcasted at 4:35 p.m. the same day.[176]

By 9:00 a.m. on Wednesday, May 6, 1931, John McCahill, Clinton "Tink" Davis and Edith Davis were being held at the Nassau County Police Department Headquarters as material witnesses. Mrs. Davis was being held on $10,000 bail; her son Tink and McCahill were held on $15,000 bail. Later, Alexander O'Neil and John Denahy—both boarders at Anna Crowley's house in Laurelton—would be held on $10,000 bail each. It was around this time that Tink, who was being held in a jail cell in the basement of police headquarters, sent word to ADA Albert DeMeo, saying that he would like to change his earlier statement. Tink told ADA DeMeo that he wasn't totally truthful earlier and he would like to set the record straight. He added that when Hirsch and Yodice drove up on them last night, he threw the loose bullets into the grass, but it was Solly who had the revolver, and he was the one who threw it into the grass behind him.[177]

At about 10:00 a.m., the recovered Ford murder vehicle was returned to Nassau County Police Headquarters for examination. Aside from the partial broken out windshield and recovered spent cartridges from inside the vehicle, it was found to have a large amount of dried human blood on the right side of the front seat. There was one bullet hole on the interior right front passenger door, with an exit bullet hole on the exterior of the same door. The vehicle was photographed and fingerprinted.[178]

At about 10:30 a.m., Detectives Brinsley and Bedell were canvassing the area around Washington Avenue and Aster Place, where taxicab driver Fowler stated that he last saw three males the night before walking with some car tires and made the report to Patrolman Yodice. Detective Bedell also stated that he had seen some tires when he initially arrived a few hours after Hirsch had been shot, but he didn't have time to investigate. They

Section of broken-out windshield in the 1930 Ford sedan Two Gun Crowley murder car. *Courtesy NCPD Homicide Squad.*

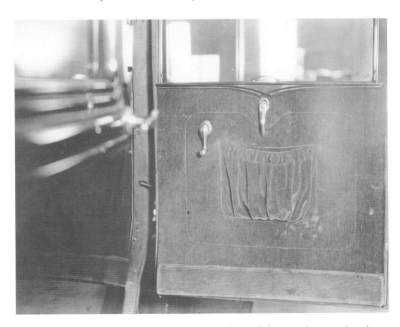

Inside view of the right front passenger car door of the murder car, showing bloodstained bullet holes that exited Patrolman Hirsch's body as he was shot fourteen times point blank, from less than four feet away as he stood between the open car door and Two Gun Crowley. *Courtesy NCPD Homicide Squad.*

happened to speak with a boy named George Balesko who lived on Astor Place, near the vacant lot where Detective Bedell had seen the tires earlier. Young George Balesko said that the tires weren't there yesterday when he went to bed, but when he got up that morning, they were there, so he took them home. The detectives took the tires from George and invoiced them as evidence at the First Precinct.[179]

At 2:45 p.m. on Wednesday, Yonkers City police chief Quirk and Lieutenant Ford were present at the NCPD headquarters to assist with the manhunt for Francis Crowley. He and his partner Rudolph Duringer were still at large and also wanted for the murder of Virginia "Joyce" Brannen ten days prior up in Yonkers.[180]

At 3:00 p.m., Sergeant Butts, an NYPD ballistic expert, was present at the NCPD headquarters and conducted a thorough examination of the recovered stolen 1930 Ford sedan. It was Butts's official opinion that the windshield was broken by gunshots coming from the inside of the vehicle to the outside, and the splintered sections of the gunshot windshield were removed by a person.[181]

By 3:33 p.m. that afternoon, Patrolman Hirsch's body had been moved to the Cornell morgue in Hempstead, New York, where an autopsy was performed by Drs. Otto Shultze and Carl Hettesheimer. Also present for the autopsy were Detective Sergeant William R. Vaughan, undertaker H.C. Penny and Nassau County Court stenographer Nat Burchel, who would be responsible for taking the official autopsy notes for court evidence. At 7:01 p.m., the completed autopsy revealed that Patrolman Hirsch had sustained three gunshot wounds to his center chest, three gunshot wounds to his right arm all just below the shoulder, two gunshot wounds to his left arm, one gunshot wound one inch above the root of the penis, three gunshot wounds to the upper right front chest just below the right scapular, one gunshot wound to the left cheek of the buttock and one gunshot wound to the left pelvis. One .38-caliber ACP bullet was removed from the fibers of the serratus muscle (thorax region); that fully jacketed bullet was rifled from right to left, base to dome, and was indented over the dome. This bullet was marked bullet no. 1 and turned over to Detective Sergeant Vaughan. On the outer side of the chest wall, at the level of the left tenth rib and in the posterior axillary line, was another .38 ACP bullet showing no deformity, rifled right to left, base to dome, with six riflings—quite dissimilar to bullet no. 1. This bullet was marked bullet no. 2 and also turned over to Vaughan. The bullets recovered belonged to the tracts of bullet wounds at entrance no. 1 and no. 2. Bullet no. 1 passed through the liver, the lower lobe of the

A daylight re-creation of the Patrolman Hirsch's murder scene for court purposes. *Courtesy NCPD Homicide Squad.*

right lung, the fractured seventh rib on the right side and the right scapula. Bullet no. 2 passed through the chest wall, the right lung, the right auricle of the heart, the liver, the stomach, the small intestine, the abdominal aorta and the left kidney. Patrolman Hirsch had been shot no less than fourteen times with a .38-caliber ACP, presumably a 128- or 130-grain bullet, from a distance no greater that four feet. There were no further bullets recovered from his body.[182]

With the brutal murder of Patrolman Hirsch, the manhunt for Two Gun Crowley intensified. His description was teletyped to every police department nationwide. Investigators knew that this cold-blooded killer had to be stopped and stopped soon before he could strike again. Every policeman in the tristate area of New York had seen his wanted poster and joined in the hunt, from the local two- and three-man rural departments to the urban NYPD with almost seventeen thousand men. New York City detectives, Yonkers City detectives, New York State Police and now Nassau County detectives were combining all their resources to flush out this murderous psycho. By sunup on Wednesday morning, every early morning newspaper from New York to California ran front-page headlines, photos and all, of the murderous cop-killing gangster Francis "Two Gun" Crowley. Two Gun Crowley was now infamous, wanted by every cop in the nation and on the lips of gossip's conversation throughout the New York area. He was the talk of the town, but nowhere more so than in North Merrick and the neighboring Roosevelt, where it all happened.[183] That's when fourteen-year-old Thelma Sinram, who lived at 23 Centennial Avenue, saw Two Gun Crowley's face on the front page of the morning newspaper and read what he did. She ran to tell her father that she knew Crowley and had spoken with him just this past week. Thelma was a pretty, petite, dark-haired girl who was as fearless as she was articulate. After hearing what Thelma had to say, her father took her straight to the detective division at police headquarters, where he knew they would be conducting interviews of any and all witnesses in their hunt for Crowley. Thelma's father was also a patrolman with the Nassau County Police Department.

Thelma was soon found to be a wealth of fresh and vital information, perhaps the only credible person capable of linking all the players together, some still unknown to the police at the time. In her statement, she told the detectives that Crowley, whom she knew by the name "Chuck" and who sometimes liked to be called "Shorty," hung out with Johnny McCahill and that McCahill had dated a girl named Elizabeth Kotz, the sister of Charlies Kotz. Elizabeth was also fourteen years old and lived on Richard Avenue off Meadowbrook Road in North Merrick, just a short walk from Black Shirt Lane. Thelma said that the last time she saw Crowley was when she had just come out of the Bohack's grocery store on Nassau Road the past Sunday, and he was just calmly leaning against his car parked at the curb, waiting for her. Thelma would go on to say that Crowley told her he was going by another name now; he was using the name "Thomas Gordon" and showed her two guns that he carried. One looked like the one her father carried (a revolver), and the other one was (automatic) flat.

She said that he was living in Southampton with a fella and a girl he knew, and he showed her a picture of the girl. Crowley told her how he had shot a New York City detective, and he asked her if she saw his picture in the paper. When she said she did, he asked her if she thought it was a good picture of him. She asked him why he shot the cop, and he said, "I've been meaning to do that for a while, to shoot a cop." Crowley also told her he hung out mostly in Merrick with the Black Shirt gang, with guys like Charlie Kotz, Johnny McCahill and Pat Dunn (no relation or connection to Billie

Dunn). But he said that he didn't really like Charlie Kotz because Kotz was a squealer, and he didn't like squealers. Thelma said she knew that Crowley would sometimes stay at the Kotzes' house, even though he "said" he didn't like Charlie. She knew that he stayed there because Elizabeth told her so and added that he told her he rode around a lot, passed by the cops all the time and the cops didn't even recognize him: "They never will, either." Thelma knew he was dating a girl named Helen Walsh who lived in the city, but Walsh came out to her bungalow on Meader Avenue in North Merrick, mostly in the summer, and they were friends with Tink, whom she knew worked at the Freeport movie theater as an usher. Thelma Sinram also gave the investigating detectives a fresher description of Crowley: he was now wearing his hair longer, and his face was much thinner, but his lower lip was thicker than could be seen in the police photos. His language and vocabulary were poor, and he had a distinctive little stutter when he talked, especially when she looked right into his eyes. Thelma said he didn't really talk like a tough guy; he actually acted very innocent. But, when she refused to go for a ride in his car, he gave her a kind of demonic smirk and abruptly broke off their conversation, got into his car and drove away.[184]

Rear view of the stolen 1930 maroon Ford sedan (murder car) operated by Two Gun Crowley. Re-creation on Black Shirt Lane by detectives after being recovered on May 7, 1931. *Courtesy NCPD Homicide Squad.*

Chief of Detectives inspector Harold King personally sifted through the inpouring of information as fast as his detectives could gather it. He even sat in on the many witness interviews conducted by the assistant district attorneys. After obtaining all the physical evidence available, combined with the written statements from the material witnesses being held in the basement of police headquarters and Thelma Sinram, he then cherry-picked what he believed to be the most relevant and viable information needed to capture this killer. Inspector King ordered his detectives to stake out the home of Crowley's foster mother in Laurelton, and he sent other detectives to Richard Avenue in North Merrick, the home of Elizabeth and Charlie Kotze. Other detectives were ordered to the home of Jerimiah Walsh, Helen's father, on Meador Avenue in North Merrick to search for Helen and for anything related to Crowley or the killing of Patrolman Hirsch. They were also to bring Jerimiah Walsh in for questioning. The NYPD Eighty-Fourth Detective Squad was notified of Helen Walsh's mother's address at 69 Nassau Street in Brooklyn, and Captain Brosman established a round-the-clock stakeout of the home in the event Helen or Crowley tried to make contact. He sent still other detectives to the Main Street home of Salvatore Russo in the village of Freeport to arrest him and bring him back to police headquarters. When any investigation becomes void of certainty, that void is usually filled by the investigators with speculation and theory; this murder was no different. For some unknown reason, Inspector King believed that Crowley had killed Helen Walsh and disposed of her body at an unknown location, perhaps in an effort to dispose of an eyewitness to Hirsch's murder. Inspector King supposedly made this assumption based partly on the blood found on the front seat of the recovered murder car and his personal theory that killers like to get rid of any witnesses. Despite that theory, Helen's friends and family said that Crowley wouldn't hurt her, that he loved her. King released his assumptions to the press.[185]

At about 6:00 p.m. on Wednesday—and after a brief low-speed car pursuit through the pastoral streets of Freeport—Detectives T. Bedell and B. Bedell arrested Salvatore Russo and brought him back to police headquarters for questioning. Russo was held as a material witnesses in Hirsch's murder and held on $15,000 bail.[186] Solly gave a written confession to Assistant District Attorney Littleton about lying to the police; he had been in possession of the silver Smith & Wesson revolver the night before and threw it to the ground when confronted by Patrolmen Hirsch and Yodice. Russo also told ADA Littleton that on April 28, the Tuesday before, he took the train from Freeport into the Bronx to meet up with Crowley. He said he met Crowley

Nassau County Police Headquarters, 1931 entrance on Fifteenth Street, Garden City, New York. *Photo courtesy NCPD museum.*

on First Avenue near the Willis Avenue bridge in upper Manhattan and Fats Duringer was with him. Russo said Crowley was driving a Chrysler Imperial sedan, and when he started to climb into the backseat, he saw thick dried blood all over the rear seat cushion. He quickly backed away from getting in the car. Russo said he asked Crowley, "What the hell happen here?" Crowley replied that he and Duringer had to kill a girl the other night. Crowley told him that he and Duringer had been paid $150 each by some uptown gang members to kill this girl from a dance hall because she knew too much about them and what they were up to and they were afraid she would go to the cops. Russo said Crowley laughed as he bragged about killing her, and he added that Crowley had a "gangster smirk" on his face and chomped on a ball of chewing gun all the while he told him the story. Both Crowley and Duringer showed Russo a big wad of cash, presumably what they had been paid to kill the girl. Crowley also added that after they shot and killed the girl, they had to dump her body up in Yonkers. Russo said he wanted no part of that and took the train back home to Freeport. He hadn't seen Crowley again until the night before.[187]

Earlier, around 11:30 a.m., Detective Pearsall left Nassau police headquarters with the bloodstained front seat cushion from Crowley's car and two full mason jars containing liver and stomach samples from Patrolman Hirsch's autopsy en route to the Cornell Clinic at 1st Avenue and 27th Street in New York City for additional analysis.[188] Detectives McClarren and B. Bedell from the Fifth Squad responded to Leo Kunoff's candy store at 38 Washington Avenue in Roosevelt to retrieve the .38-caliber bullet Crowley had previously shot into the floor according to the witness statement of Howard Singer. The bullet couldn't be found, as it passed through the wood, landing somewhere in the dirt floor of the basement.[189]

Late Wednesday afternoon, after gathering all the information and intelligence he had obtained from the various witness statements, Inspector King sent Assistant District Attorney Spoor, Chief of Police Quirk and Detective Sergeant Kearney to Southampton, New York, in the police department's four-seat Stinson airplane in search of Crowley. The plane was piloted by civilian pilot Randy Enslow. They met with Southampton police chief Lane, who was unable to provide anything or anyone to assist them in their search. Detective Sergeant Kearney then went to meet with Suffolk County deputy sheriff Goodale in Riverhead. ADA Spoor and Chief Quirk flew back to police headquarters in Mineola before dark, as Enslow was not

Nassau County police airplane that was used to hunt down Two Gun Crowley and Helen Walsh after the murder of Patrolman Fred S. Hirsch Jr. *Courtesy NCPD museum.*

qualified to fly at night. Meanwhile, Kearney and Goodale drove out to the village of Greenport, on the north fork of Long Island, to investigate a report that persons answering Helen Walsh's and Crowley's description had been seen in the Greenport area. That report was unfounded. Kearney returned to Riverhead and met with Deputy Sheriff Taylor, who drove Kearney to the Lyng estate in Southampton, where he interviewed John Olderfield, who was a member of the lathers' union in New York City. Olderfield stated that he knew Crowley but had never seen him anywhere around Southampton. Kearney notified Inspector King by telephone, and he returned to police headquarters by the Long Island Railroad. District Attorney Edwards was so confident in Inspector King's intelligence—largely based on a fourteen-year-old girl's statement, which had been completely fueled by the gangster himself—that Crowley was hiding out in Southampton, he gave a press release: "Suffolk County is very broad and very wide, and I'm betraying no secret when I say we feel we have our man located within that county."[190]

Crowley would later laugh as he testified; "he sure gave the cops the runaround," sending them to Southampton. He also added that he would make things up to see who was a rat and might give him up to the cops.[191]

11

The Siege

On May 7, the Nassau County Patrolman's Benevolent Association voted to give Patrolman Hirsch's wife, Freda, and his four children $500. It also offered a reward of $2,500 to anyone for Crowley's capture. District Attorney Edwards said he would also ask the Nassau County Board of Supervisors to offer an additional $5,000 and expected other groups to raise the total of the rewards to $15,000.[192]

Meanwhile, there was still no trace of Helen Walsh, and newspapers speculated that she had met the same fate as Virginia Brannen at the hands of Crowley. Evidence found in the abandoned murder car had suggested that she had been killed by Crowley, according to Inspector King.[193] Helen's mother spoke to a reporter: "Frank Crowley is a splendid young man, no matter what people say about him being a murderer! He is madly in love with my daughter, I don't believe he has killed her. He'll bring her home to me, unharmed, I know he would rather die than see anything happen to Helen."[194]

But Helen's father wasn't so certain, he told District Attorney Edwards: "If that little rat has done anything to my little girl, I'll kill him with my own hands! He didn't give Hirsch a chance. He won't give you one, so if you find him, let him have it—before he gets you!"[195]

From Thursday, April 30, to Thursday, May 7, Crowley spent less than two complete days out of the seven at that fifth-floor walkup apartment on West 90th Street in Manhattan. His sporadic appearance at the West 90th Street hideout was more out of desperation, or as a last resort; he had no other place to go. He made the long trip back and forth from North Merrick on Long Island one last time before he became trapped like a cornered rat. Duringer was the exception; he stayed in the apartment without Crowley. Even when Billie Dunn went off to the Primrose Club, he stayed behind. It might have been out of loyalty to Crowley, like a good soldier awaiting further orders, but most likely, he was just a lazy, unmotivated drunken killer.[196]

Helen Walsh would later take Nassau district attorney Elvin Edwards, Inspector King and police matron Mrs. Louis Schwab on a guided tour, retracing their escape route after Crowley gunned down Patrolman Hirsch. Helen said she lay in the dark on the floor in the backseat of the car until Crowley got on to Washington Avenue: "Then we turned onto to Park Avenue, then to Roosevelt Avenue, then on to Nassau Road, then we followed Nassau Road to the north side of the Southern Parkway, and along the parkway into Queens."[197] She remembered Crowley stopping the car and breaking the windshield out on the right side. He changed the license plates and reloaded his two guns. Shorty then drove the car to the Long Island Railroad train station in Jamaica and parked the car. They took a cab to Long Island City, got out of the car, walked three or four blocks and took another cab to West 90th Street in Manhattan.

Helen recounted that when they got to Shorty's apartment on West 90th Street, his old girlfriend Billie Dunn was still there, and so was Fats Duringer. It was late, and they were sleeping. She said that Shorty had telephoned Billie Dunn earlier and told her, "You better clear out, I'm bringing a real girl home to the apartment. You can go with Duringer."[198] Helen said that when they got to the apartment, Crowley took her into the bedroom that he had shared with Billie. Billie was asleep, but Crowley woke her up by kicking the side of the bed and told her again to get out of the apartment. Billie got up and, in disbelief, just stood there staring at Helen. Billie then gave Helen the 1931 version of the stink eye. Crowley hauled off and punched Billie right in the face and told her to go sleep with Fats in the other bedroom, because he and Helen were taking this bedroom.[199] Later in the evening, around 8:00 p.m. on May 6, as the massive manhunt for Crowley was being ratchetted up by the tens of thousands of New York police, Crowley took Helen down to the East Village in Manhattan for dinner and dancing while Billie Dunn went to the Primrose Club to work. Fats stayed behind in the apartment.[200]

When Billie got to the Primrose later that night, she was so angry with Crowley that she told all the other dancers what that dirty dog did to her, and she told anyone who would listen that he had moved his new girlfriend into the apartment along with that fat friend of his, Duringer. One of the other dancers seized on this information, knowing that there was a reward for Crowley and Duringer, and quietly called the police at the Forty-Second Detective Squad. She gave the information to Detectives Caso and Mara—only thing was, she didn't know the location of Billie Dunn's apartment. The hardboiled city detectives Caso and Mara had to search for an address.[201] Around the same time, Nassau County detectives Joseph Culkin and George Hutchinson were informed by Chief of Detectives inspector Harold King that he had received a telephone call from a Detective Mullee at the NYPD Eighteenth Squad on West 47th Street in Manhattan. A taxicab driver named John Sharp of 420 East 155th in Manhattan called in with information on Crowley's whereabouts. A skeptical Inspector King reluctantly dispatched Culkin and Hutchinson to the Eighteenth Squad. The taxi driver said he was positive that the guy he picked up as a fare the past Sunday, May 3, at around midnight was, in fact, Two Gun Crowley. He asked to be taken to Brooklyn, but when they reached Brooklyn, without ever getting out of the cab, Crowley asked to be taken to Jamaica. From Jamaica, Crowley asked to be driven to a private house on 113th Street and Liberty Avenue in Ozone Park. Sharp assured Detectives Culkin and Hutchinson that he could show them the exact house where finally dropped Crowley off at in Ozone Park.[202]

As Nassau detectives Culkin and Hutchinson and NYPD detective Mullee were about to leave with Sharpe, Detectives Barry and Sheehan from NYPD's Fortieth Squad called and asked them to wait a couple of minutes, as they would like to take the ride with them out to Ozone Park. At 3:45 p.m., when Detectives Barry and Sheehan arrived at the Eighteenth Squad, just as they were are all about to leave, Detective Barry received a telephone call from Detective Caso in the Forty-Second Squad informing them that he had just located an address for Billie Dunn's apartment on West 90th Street. Everyone was to meet at 610 West End Avenue and 89th Street, around the corner from the address, to hash out a tactical approach to apprehend Crowley.[203] At about 4:15 p.m., Inspector Bruckner from the Bronx detective headquarters arrived with Detective Byrnes, and after discreetly showing photos to a few citizens in the area, they determined that Billie Dunn's apartment was number 10, on the top floor of the five-story apartment building at 303 West 90th Street.

Apartment 10 was a small two-bedroom, one-bath flat with a narrow galley kitchen, all connecting by one hallway. The bedroom windows faced the back of the building and overlooked a small courtyard. The detectives

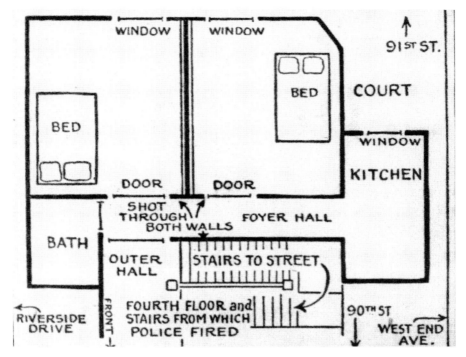

Diagram of apartment 10 on the (fifth) top floor of 303 West 90th Street, where Crowley, Duringer and Walsh staged their spectacular gun battle against the police on May 7, 1931. *Courtesy of the* New York Daily News.

also determined that persons fitting Crowley's, Walsh's and Duringer's descriptions might presently be in that fifth-floor apartment. Detective Mara was well acquainted with this location and various apartment buildings in the area. To blend in with a makeshift disguise, he dressed as a plumber, and Detective Sheehan used the disguise of a laborer. Detectives Byrnes, Barry and Hutchinson somehow managed to obtain three suitcases and covered as traveling salesmen, making use of the vacant apartment across the hall from Crowley's. Detective Culkin was to take up a position on the stairway between the fourth and fifth floor to prevent their escapes.[204] Time was of the essence, and they needed the element of surprise to prevent any unnecessary casualties. With no time to go from door to door to evacuate the other inhabitants of the building, Inspector Bruckner notified his command and requested additional police backup.

The detectives quietly moved into their assigned positions and awaited the prearranged diversionary (pipe banging) signal from Detective

Mara. With the sound of Mara's signal, it didn't take long for Crowley and Duringer to curiously exit their apartment. With guns drawn, they carefully walked around the lightless fifth-floor hallway at the top of the stairs, looking down to see what was causing all the pipe banging and heavy footsteps they could hear on the stairs. Detective Mara was on the fourth floor, hidden from view, banging on the exposed pipes that ran vertically along the outside walls of the stairwell between all five floors to draw out any occupants in apartment 10.[205] As Crowley and Duringer peered over the top of the wooden banister to see where the noise was coming from, they either saw something that didn't look right to them or the paranoia that came from being hunted by every cop in New York heightened their flight senses, and they quickly backed away from the railing and jumped back into their apartment. The seven detectives, who were now separated by the building's interior stairway, had no way to communicate other than by an occasional eye contact or hand gesturing. Anything more overt could expose them to the fugitives. Detective Byrnes took the initial action, and as soon as Crowley jumped back into the apartment, but before he could close the door, Byrnes quietly opened the door of apartment 11 a crack and immediately started firing. Crowley quickly closed his door, and he and Duringer responded to Detective Byrnes with their own volley of bullets. Crowley directed his fire through the wall of the hallway into apartment 11 while Duringer fired into the stairway toward the fourth floor. Detectives Sheehan, Culkin, Caso and Mara, who were on the floor below, were forced back around the stairwell for cover. When Crowley and Duringer stopped shooting, Sheehan, Caso, Mara and Culkin slowly advanced around the stairway with their backs to the wall while laying down a combined line of gunfire up into Crowley's apartment. They creeped forward in an effort to keep the fugitives contained in the apartment while Detectives Byrnes, Barry and Hutchinson continued to fire at the door and walls.[206]

With a momentary lull in the shooting, detectives yelled, "Crowley come out or we're going to kill you!" Crowley just responded, "Come and get me copper!"[207] As the steady stream of gunshots continued, the NYPD Emergency Service Squad (ESS) arrived. The ESS is a highly trained elite unit that the cops call when they need help. They were followed by no fewer than about two hundred other patrolman and detectives who quickly surrounded the building on West 90th Street. It was later described as the largest and longest gunfight siege that Manhattan had ever seen and would become known as the "Siege of 90th Street."[208]

With every means of escape cut off—fire escapes, hallways and windows—Crowley had no choice but to shoot it out with the cops, and he didn't want it any other way. Emergency Service cops were dispatched to the roof of 303. On neighboring rooftops, police sharpshooters took up lofty positions to take out Crowley and his crew given the opportunity. Machine gun–toting police covered the rear of Crowley's building from the courtyard with a limited view of the only two windows in the apartment. As the police moved into their positions in the courtyard, which had limited cover, Crowley and Duringer haphazardly rained down lead from the windows above. The police responded with heavy machine-gun fire. The ESS police on top of 303 started chopping holes into Crowley's apartment bedroom ceiling. As a sporadic volley of shots poured up through the roof at them, the police backed away, then resumed hacking at the roof as the courtyard machine-gun fire drew Crowley's attention away from them. They cut their way through two roof openings, one in each bedroom. At times, Crowley could be seen running from window to window between the bedrooms with guns blazing in both hands. He was shooting through the walls, up through the ceiling and out through the windows. He was busy, and he was outnumbered. He had concerns on several fronts: the door to the apartment covered by the detectives in apartment 11, the neighboring rooftop sharpshooters and the cops above on his own roof throwing teargas bombs inside. The police would later find five handguns in the apartment, which would explain how he seemed never to run out of ammo.[209] Helen later admitted to reloading the guns for Crowley and Duringer as they shot it out with the police. When it was all over, the police counted the bullet holes in the small apartment's walls, doors and even the furniture. They stopped when they reached seven hundred, but there were many more.[210]

Uniformed patrolman arrived and began handing long guns up to the detectives holed up on the interior stairs. Armed with heavier firepower, the detectives on the stairs began to fire at Crowley and his crew through the banister spindles and penetrated the door and walls of the apartment. The police sharpshooters fired at Crowley and Duringer when they saw the duo dart across the shot-out windows; other cops maintained steady machine-gun fire whenever they saw movement through the apartment windows.[211] The Emergency Service cops on the apartment roof lit the fuses for teargas bombs and threw them in—some of these Crowley threw back out the window at the police in the courtyard before they had a chance to ignite and release the teargas inside the apartment. The teargas bombs had seven-second fuses; it didn't take more than two or three seconds for Crowley or

Crowd of spectators gather on 90th Street outside of apartment building number 303 while the police continued their armed assault on the fifth floor to apprehend Crowley, Duringer and Walsh on May 7, 1931. *Courtesy of the* New York Daily News.

Duringer to throw them at the vulnerable cops below in the courtyard. For every teargas bomb Crowley hurled back at the police, the police threw another two into the apartment.[212] (**NYPD** commissioner Mulrooney later ordered that fuse lengths on teargas bombs be changed to three-second fuses. They studied the feasibility of a teargas bomb that would burst on contact, requiring no fuse detonation.[213]) Soon the fog of teargas engulfed the entire fifth floor of the building and started cascading down the stairway to the floors below, enveloping the detectives on the stairway as well as some of the cops in the courtyard. The crowd of spectators in the street continued to grow; it was soon estimated that the number of onlookers had surpassed ten thousand. Word spread that the gangster Francis "Two Gun" Crowley was shooting it out with the police. The sound of gunshots could be heard for blocks around. It echoed between the buildings as the siege continued. New York City police commissioner Mulroney eventually responded and led the siege. He later described it as the "most thrilling and dramatic experience" he had ever had in his thirty years as a police officer.[214]

12

Captured

When sixteen-year-old Helen wasn't reloading Crowley's guns, during the few brief times there was a lull in the shooting, she had time to reflect, as did her boyfriend. She even had time to pen a couple quick notes to leave behind, which the police found after the siege:

To whom it may concern

I was born on the 13th of October, and he was born on the 31st. If I die and my face you are able to see, wave my hair, and make me look pretty and make my face up. Dress me in a black and white new dress. Do my nails all over, don't use this kind of polish it's too dark, I use pale pink. I always wanted everybody to be happy and have a good time—I had some pretty good times myself.
Love to all but all my love to sweets
P.S. Everybody be happy now
Helen Walsh[215]

In another, Helen actually defended Crowley:

Everyone thinks he is hard he can't be hard when he cooked my breakfast and washed a pair of pajamas so I could sleep in them. The only thing I regret is that I will not see the rest of the world. I always wanted to travel.

P.S. Show this to my sister so she will know I died singing, please don't talk about me while I'm gone.[216]

Helen even had time to write a brief note for Crowley. He dictated it to her, though it appears she may have added a line or two of her own;

To whom it may concern:

I was born on the 31ˢᵗ. She was born on the 13ᵗʰ. I guess it was fate that made us meet. When I die put a lily in my hand and let the boys know how they'll look. Underneath my coat will lie a weary heart what wouldn't harm anybody. I had nothing else to do, that's why I went around bumping off cops. It is a new sensation of its own. Take a tip from me to never let a copper go an inch above your knee. They tell you that they love you, but as soon as you turn your back, they'll club you and say "what the hell."

The police also intercepted two letters Helen had written to her mother the day before. Crowley had taken the subway to Brooklyn to mail them in an attempt to throw the cops off his trail. The letter said, in part,

Dear Mom:

I'm all right and don't worry about me. I am being taken care of. We were married today. He is taking me to Canada tonight. We were not petting [necking, or making out]. *We were sitting there talking and Shorty was afraid I would get shot and that's why he got away. Tell Olive* [Helen's sister] *not to worry about me.*

They didn't really get married; however, they did display rings on the ring finger of their left hands. These were purely props for the landlord, as the early twentieth-century culture frowned on respectable landlords renting an apartment to an unmarried couple. Helen wanted her mother to continue to think of her as a wholesome young woman, to believe she wasn't hosting a petting party with the cop-killing gangster the night before. But shooting cops didn't seem to be an insalubrious exploit.[217]

About two hours into the siege, after the hallway door and walls of Crowley's apartment had been riddled with bullets, the teargas became unbearable, and the police continued to pump bullets into the apartment. They heard Crowley call out, "We give up! We give up! We're out of bullets.

Don't hurt the girl." With that, the detectives rushed to the top floor and NYPD detective Johnny Broderick broke the apartment door down with an axe. Detectives Sheehan, Byrnes and Culkin rushed into the first bedroom and grabbed Crowley, who was lying half on a bed that was overturned and half on the floor. Byrnes grabbed Crowley's legs, while Sheehan grabbed his hands. Detective Byrnes found a .32-caliber automatic pistol and a .38-caliber automatic pistol tied to each of Crowley's leg by two white pieces of cloth. Both guns were fully loaded.[218]

Detective Culkin searched Crowley and found a large quantity of bullets in his pockets. Crowley was bleeding from wounds on both his wrists and ankles. Crowley was carried down to a first-floor apartment, where he was strip-searched and a doctor tended to his wounds. He was then taken by a gurney to a waiting ambulance. Meanwhile, Hutchinson and the other detectives searched through the thick cloud of choking teargas and found Duringer uninjured and hiding under the bed in the other bedroom. Walsh was also found uninjured and hiding in an upright wardrobe in the same bedroom. Crowley was taken by ambulance under heavy guard to Bellevue Hospital, while Duringer and Walsh were taken to NYPD headquarters for questioning.[219] A few minutes before Crowley's surrender, a Fox News cameraman on his way to another assignment heard the police sirens and decided to follow them. This detour led to the creation of one of the first dramatic live crime films ever made.[220]

A wounded Two Gun Crowley is wheeled out on a gurney from 303 West 90th Street after his two-hour gun battle with the police ended. *Library of Congress.*

They hadn't even reached police headquarters before Duringer started confessing to his shooting and killing of Virginia Brannen the week before. Helen at least waited until they reached police headquarters before she told Nassau district attorney Elvin Edwards and Inspector Harold King how she watched Crowley gun down Patrolman Hirsch. Helen was informed that if she cooperated with the prosecution and testified against Crowley, any and all charges against her would be dropped—provided, of course, that Crowley was convicted of first-degree murder.[221] Helen agreed and was taken into protective custody by Edwards and transported back to Nassau County, where she was sequestered at an unknown location, pending a grand jury inquiry into the death of Patrolman Hirsch. Rudolph Duringer provided the Yonkers and New York City detectives a detailed confession to the events leading up to Virginia's murder, and his motive. Duringer also said that he killed Virginia on Jerome Avenue in the Bronx and confirmed that he and Crowley had disposed of her body in Yonkers. With this confession, Duringer was transferred from the Manhattan Tombs detention facility to the Bronx County Jail, pending the Bronx County Grand Jury.[222]

At 2:40 p.m. on Friday, May 8, Francis "Two Gun" Crowley was discharged from Bellevue Hospital in New York City and transported by ambulance to police headquarters in Mineola. In the rear of the ambulance with Crowley were Nassau district attorney Elvin Edwards and Inspector Harold King, there to listen to Crowley's boisterous, immature and, at times, imaginary account of his murderous career of crime for the entire trip. An escort shadowed the ambulance to Nassau headquarters, where a crowd of young people gathered to await a glimpse of a real gangster, Two Gun Crowley.[223] The crowd was estimated to be as large as two thousand as they converged on Fifteenth Street between police headquarters and the county courthouse. Most were excited teenage girls who instantly swarmed around the ambulance as it pulled up to the curb, prompting a detail of uniformed police to create an armed linked barrier around the ambulance. Crowley was booked inside the vehicle.[224] Sergeant Philips noted Crowley's pedigree in the large book, and then he was taken under guard to the Nassau Hospital in Mineola, where he was admitted and treated for superficial gunshot wounds by Dr. Carl Hettesheimer, the same doctor who performed the autopsy on Patrolman Hirsch just two days earlier.[225] Later, when DA Edwards visited Crowley at the hospital, he asked, "What can I do to make you comfortable?" Crowley replied, "I'm pretty hungry, I'd like a good meal." Mr. Edwards then offered, "How about a nice steak, if the doctor will let you have it?" Crowley replied in a chastising tone, "You forget that this is Friday. You can't eat meat on Friday!"[226]

Earlier that morning, a grand jury was impaneled at the Nassau County Courthouse in Mineola to hear testimony in the matter of the murder of Patrolman Fred Hirsch Jr. Presenting the case before the grand jury was DA Elvin Edwards himself, which galvanized the importance and priority of the presentation. In addition to the required witnesses—Patrolman Peter Yodice, medical experts, firearms experts and the investigating

A 1931 photo of the Nassau County Court House located on Franklin Avenue in Mineola, New York, where Crowley was indicted by the grand jury on May 8, 1931, and where his murder trial started on May 25, 1931. *Courtesy of the Nassau County Photo Archive Center.*

detectives—was DA Edwards's star eyewitness, Crowley's sixteen-year-old girlfriend Helen Walsh. Only nine witnesses, including Helen, were called to testify. Other than her background information, Helen's testimony wasn't longer than five full minutes. She stated:

> *Sure he* [Crowley] *shot Hirsch, the policeman didn't have a chance. He killed him because he thought the cop recognized him. He thought he was caught. Hirsch said to him, "Let me see your driver's license." Then he pulled out his guns and started firing. I don't know how many shots he fired; I was scared stiff. Then he reached across the seat and pushed the cop's body off the running board, but not before taking the cop's gun from his holster. Then he said to me, "Baby, that's the way to treat a cop. I guess I fixed him up all right, didn't I?"*

Helen further stated that when Hirsch approached the car, "he was very polite. The other cop Yodice was not, he was rough and angry like." "It's too bad the nice cop was killed," she added. After Helen finished her testimony, DA Edwards informed the grand jurors about the content of the law and exited the room, allowing the jurors to vote in secrecy. A total of twenty-two minutes lapsed from the beginning testimony of the first witness

The grand jury's star witnesses against Two Gun Crowley was sixteen-year-old Helen Walsh, pictured here sandwiched between Nassau detective Patrick Shanley and Nassau County police matron Mrs. Louis Schwab, as she nervously awaits her turn in the secret proceedings against her murderous boyfriend. *Courtesy of the* Brooklyn Times Union.

to when the grand jury foreman handed up its true bill for an indictment against Francis Crowley, for murder in the first degree. This set a new county record for the fastest murder indictment in the court's history.[227]

Meanwhile, justice was moving just as swiftly inside the Bronx County Supreme Court house as Duringer was indicted for the murder of Virginia Brannen. Duringer's indictment was almost as quick as Crowley's, with an almost guaranteed certainty based on his confession to the police and supported by Robert LeClair's account.[228] On Thursday, the day before the grand jury, Duringer awoke starved from a restful night's sleep on the hard wooden bed in the detention cells at NYPD headquarters and hungrily ordered a breakfast of pork chops and coffee. After eating his breakfast and a short nap, Duringer reiterated his confession and took Detectives

Caso and Mara on a guided tour of the murder route through the Bronx up into Yonkers, where he and Crowley dumped Virginia's body. Duringer also pinpointed the exact location where he had shot Virginia on Jerome Avenue under the elevated rail system at 212th Street. He remembered it well because he remembered seeing a tombstone establishment on the corner.[229] In Duringer's initial confession to NYPD assistant chief inspector Sullivan, when asked by Inspector Sullivan, "Did you kill Virginia Brannen?" Duringer replied, "Yes, I shot her because I loved her." Inspector Sullivan then said, "Tell us about the night of the killing." Duringer replied in detail:

> *Well, after the dance club closed, we got into the car. Crowley was driving, and Robert LeClair and Mildred Moore were in the front seat with him. Virginia and I sat on the backseat. We stopped at a speakeasy on 125th Street and had something to eat and some drinks, then got back into the car and drove through the Bronx. While driving through the Bronx, Virginia told me she didn't love me anymore and she was going to marry someone else, so I shot her.*

Inspector Sullivan then asked, "Did you shoot her right after she told you she was going to marry someone else?" Duringer admitted, "No, I thought it over for about three minutes and then I shot her. I had one of Crowley's guns in my pocket. My hand felt it, and I decided I would kill her right there in the car. The noise of the overhead trains would drown out the shot. I'm sorry I shot her." Duringer continued with his confession of the events after he and Crowley dumped her body. They returned to the Bronx, and he and Crowley had fought off the cops on West 90th Street. After being arraigned on the charge of murder in the first degree before the Honorable Judge Albert Cohn, in the Bronx County Supreme Court, Duringer was held for trial.[230]

In New York in 1931, a conviction of murder in the first degree carried an automatic death sentence, with the main element of the crime being the premeditated act of killing someone, a deliberately planned act in advance. So, with Duringer stating in his confession that he shot and killed Virginia not out of a sudden white heat of passion because she didn't love him anymore, but with a cold and calculated deliberation of three full minutes, was all that was needed to seal his fate for an indictment of murder in the first degree.

At 10:00 a.m. on Saturday, May 8, under heavy police guard at the Nassau Hospital in Mineola, Crowley had a rare weekend bedside arraignment for his record-breaking indictment for murder in the first degree by the

Francis "Two Gun" Crowley's Nassau County arrest fingerprints, compared and certified as belonging to the same prisoner being transferred and accepted at Sing Sing Prison on June 1, 1931. *Courtesy Sing Sing Prison.*

Honorable Lewis J. Smith of the Nassau County Court. In attendance was Nassau County district attorney Elvin N. Edwards. The ten-minute bedside arraignment for the murder of Patrolman Hirsch held Crowley over for trial with no bail or bond. The court informed Crowley he could enter only a plea of not guilty based on the charge of the indictment and assigned him legal counsel, Charles R. Weeks. A trial date of May 11, the following Monday, was scheduled, less than forty-eight hours away.[231] Weeks agreed to represent Crowley, provided he be granted sufficient time to prepare a defense for his new client. Justice Smith was agreeable with Weeks's request and afforded him two additional weeks. The trial was now rescheduled for Monday, May 25, which DA Edwards accepted. It was an interesting, and perhaps unusual, lineup of legal minds, if not an outright phenomenal occurrence by today's standards. Notwithstanding any political connections, Crowley's legal counsel, the prosecution and Justice Smith had all had been elected district attorneys of Nassau County. Judge Lewis J. Smith served as the Nassau County DA from 1914 to 1916, Charles R. Weeks from 1917 to 1925 and Elvin Edwards from 1926 to 1934, an unbroken chain of twenty years between them.[232]

While Crowley was being arraigned by Justice Lewis Smith in the Mineola Hospital, a full inspector's funeral was being held in Bellmore for slain patrolman Fred S. Hirsch Jr. At 10:00 a.m., Patrolman Hirsch's body was escorted from his home at 305 Hicks Street to Saint Barnabas Roman Catholic Church by over one thousand police officers, including almost all the members of the NCPD and a number of visiting police. Thousands of community members also gathered in front of the Hirsch home to pay their respects as his coffin was carried out, followed by his wife and children.[233] A full requiem Mass was conducted by the Reverend John Wynne at Saint Barnabas's Catholic Church, which was only a short walk from the Hirsch family home. A remorseful and sad Patrolman Peter Yodice's shoulders shook, as his sobs were heard throughout the crammed church. Finally, when he could bear his grief no longer, he quickly left the church. Nassau County police chaplain Francis Healy of Garden City placed his hand on the coffin and said, "Greater love hath no man than this—he gave his life for his partner." Reverend Healy continued with the eulogy to a packed church:

Fred Hirsch was a real policeman. He was a perfect policeman. His one thought was of his wife, his children and his home. It has been said that he died with his murderer's name on his lips. If he did, you can rest assured it was a prayer and not a curse, for he was courageous and strong.

Over one thousand police and neighbors watch as murdered Nassau County patrolman Fred S. Hirsch Jr.'s casket is removed from the rear of undertaker C.S. Bartholomew's hearse and carried into Saint Barnabas the Apostle Roman Catholic Church on Bedford Avenue in Bellmore, New York, on May 9, 1931. *Courtesy of the* New York Daily News.

At the close of the eulogy, the casket was carried to a hearse laden with exquisite wreaths and sprays of flowers as the police band played "Nearer My God to Thee."[234]

13

Swift Justice

L ate in the evening on Saturday May 9, Crowley was discharged from the prison ward of the Mineola Hospital and transported under heavy police escort to the Nassau County Jail, which was located just behind the Nassau County Courthouse on Franklin Avenue in Mineola.[235] Crowley's superficial gunshot wounds would continue to heal in jail, while his legal counsel prepared his defense. The county jail and the county courthouse were conveniently connected by a subterranean tunnel system that allowed prisoners to be escorted between the two buildings without being exposed to either the media or general public.[236] It was an added safety feature for the escorting sheriffs and a deterrent should someone attempt to interfere with an escort or a prisoner try an escape. A fresh rumor circulated among other inmates at the county jail that the famous gangster was planning a crash out, though the rumor provided no further details. But the police and the sheriff's department weren't taking any chances that he would make some spectacular attempt at escaping. In most murder cases of the time, a single officer would sit beside the defendant in court. With Crowley, there were four, two uniformed police officers and two deputy sheriffs within an arm's reach. In addition, there were ten officers stationed throughout the courtroom, with another three police officers at the door.[237]

On Monday, May 25, at 10:00 a.m., with Crowley seated at the defense table, DA Edwards and Weeks stood before Justice Smith and informed the court they were ready for trial. The small first-floor courtroom was packed with spectators, reporters and off-duty police. The trial also attracted an unusually large throng of curiosity seekers; most were young boys and girls, all of whom were too young to attend the proceedings. Two Gun Crowley had also become the romantic object of many a female admirer, both young and old. The jail reported that he was receiving large wads of mail from worshipful women.[238] One wealthy Long Island woman had her six-year-old daughter deliver him a bunch of sweet violets while she waited in her limousine mid-block on Fifteenth Street away from the county jail.[239]

Charles Weeks, Crowley's court-appointed attorney, was first to address the court. He made a motion seeking a change of venue to an upstate location, arguing that his client would be unable to receive a fair trial in any Nassau County court because of the Fox newsreels of the siege on 90th Street and his capture in New York City, given the widespread negative attention it had received. Justice Smith quickly dismissed the motion and ordered both sides to begin the jury selection.[240] It was an unseasonable hot and muggy May for Long Island, with the temperature soaring to the eighty-eight-degree mark by midafternoon of the first day.[241] The south-facing side of the little courtroom was a series of high double-hung windows overlooking fifteenth street and a panoramic view of the police department's new headquarters across the treelined street. The open windows and two floor fans placed in the corners at the rear of the courtroom did little to cool the overpacked courtroom. In the first two and half hours of the jury selection, the court witnessed bitter prejudice against the pint-sized police slayer, which bogged down the entire selection. One by one, a parade of seventy-five prospective jurors took to the stand and stated that they had already formed an opinion on Crowley's guilt.

When the court adjourned at 1:00 p.m. for lunch, only five jurors had been selected. The afternoon session proved as fruitful, with the first ten potential jurors examined and dismissed in eight minutes. Of the one hundred jurors paneled, only five had been selected by the end of the day. The court instructed the sheriff to panel another one hundred for the next day.[242] Crowley appeared at times to be bored with the whole process, and at other times, he took an active role in the jury selection. He became the final arbiter in some of Tuesday's selection. Twenty-three times he ordered a prospect rejected. He told Weeks, "Nix on that guy, he looks like a cop"; "Nothing doing, that guy looks too slick"; "Outside with that bum, he'd hang his own grandmother"; even "What, with that jaw! Not a chance"; and "He's lying when he says he hasn't got an opinion already, Can him! Can him! I don't like him." At one point, Crowley seemed tickled with the proceedings, as he kept grinning and chawing away with his mouth full of chewing gum. The only evidence of the gunshot wounds he received was a slight limp when he walked. He made no effort to show off, other than to give his attorney a dejected frown as he turned a thumbs down to a potential juror being grilled on the witness stand. Weeks quickly dismissed the juror while Crowley slowly turned and looked around the courtroom, giving everyone his shifty smirk. Crowley evidenced no realization of the severity of the criminal charge against him; he even seemed pleased with himself for all the excitement he had generated. [243]

By Tuesday afternoon, 12 jurors acceptable to both sides had been selected—out of a pool of 275—prompting Justice Smith to openly remark, "In all my experience I have never seen a panel exhausted with such celerity."[244] The all-male jury consisted of Henry C. Comings (foreman) from Manhasset, William H. Mitchell from Locust Valley, Harold Crawford from Williston Park, Adolph Koterman from Floral Park, Wallace B Willis from Floral Park, Ernest A. Schulz from Farmingdale, Anthony Schumann from Freeport, John F. Duncombe from Lawrence, Joseph H. Schaad from Port Washington, Charles H. Eckelkamp from Floral Park, Andrew W. Gibson from Garden City and Henry Carpenter from Hempstead.

The opening remarks followed, with DA Elvin Edwards informing the jurors that he would prove beyond a shadow of a doubt, that the defendant's actions were premeditated. Crowley wasn't acting in self-defense, as he had claimed in his earlier statements made to the police, nor was he insane at the time he killed Patrolman Hirsch. Crowley was a fugitive on the run from justice, and in order to escape, he killed a policeman in cold blood. DA Edwards would further relate to the jurors that they would be hearing testimony from creditable and truthful witnesses, some of whom were the defendant's own friends, even his own girlfriend. Plus, there was undisputable evidence that the defendant had harbored an earnest desire to kill a policeman. DA Edwards concluded his opening statement to the jurors: "We ask a first-degree verdict, and the electric chair!"[245] Crowley just glanced over to the jurors and flashed them his gangster smirk as DA Edwards took his seat.[246] Weeks, Crowley's defense attorney, relayed to the jurors and the court that even though Crowley confessed to the police that he killed Patrolman Hirsch, he would prove that Crowley wasn't responsible for his acts, that Hirsch's killing wasn't a premeditated act. Weeks further asserted he would prove that Crowley had the mentality of a ten-year-old— he was just a scared kid when he shot Patrolman Hirsch. The attorney wasn't seeking to free Crowley but to have him permanently incarcerated in jail or an insane asylum rather than put to death.[247]

Above, left: Nassau County district attorney (1926–1934) Elvin N. Edwards, who personally prosecuted Francis "Two Gun" Crowley for the murder of Patrolman Fred S. Hirsch Jr. *Courtesy of the Nassau County District Attorney's office.*

Above, right: Charles R. Weeks (Nassau County district attorney, 1917–1925), court-appointed attorney for Francis "Two Gun" Crowley. *Courtesy of the Nassau County District Attorney's Office.*

Left: Honorable Lewis J. Smith, who presided over Francis "Two Gun" Crowley's murder trial. *Courtesy of the Nassau County Photo Archive Center.*

Because the burden of proof in any criminal case rests with the (state) prosecution, the prosecution presents its case to the court first. So, late on Tuesday afternoon of May 26, DA Edwards called his first witness: Patrolman Yodice. Yodice was a husky rookie who had served only four months with the Nassau County Police Department. Yodice testified under direct examination nothing significantly different from his written statement to the district attorney on the morning of Wednesday, May 6. Yodice did not recognize Crowley as being the wanted New York City gangster when he had shone his flashlight into his face that night. He further stated that he only went into the bushes when heard the gunfire because he couldn't get his gun out of the holster. Yodice's direct testimony was relatively short and less taxing compared to the severe grilling he took from Weeks on the cross-examination.

Yodice testified under cross-examination that he had very little firearms instruction from the police department. When Weeks asked, "Isn't it true that you ran away when you heard the gunshots? Yodice replied, "No, I didn't run. I backed away."

"Didn't your partner call to you for help, and didn't you refuse to aid him?"

"No, I did the best I could for him. I couldn't get my gun out in time, and I stayed in the bushes until I did. I didn't hear him yell for me."

"What did he yell then?"

"He yelled O-O-O." This would later be contradicted by Helen Walsh's testimony. She said she heard Hirsch yell something like "Yodice, Yodice," as he was slumping to the ground under Crowley's gunfire. Justice Smith adjourned for the day.[248]

Wednesday, May 27, day number three, DA Edwards called NYPD Bronx homicide detective Edward Byrnes for the first witness of the day. Detective Byrnes described the epic gun battle to the jury. Complete with teargas bombs and over two hundred of his fellow officers, the assault climaxed after almost two hours with the successful capture of Two Gun Crowley. Crowley had lied about being out of bullets when he surrendered; he actually had two fully loaded guns tied to his legs when he was taken into custody.[249] NYPD detective William C. Mara testified that he and his partner, Detective Dominic Caso, had been hunting for Crowley for the shooting of Detective Schaedel since March 13.[250] The next two witnesses were Dr. Karl Hettesheimer, the medical examiner who performed the autopsy on Patrolman Hirsch, and Dr. Otto Schiltze, who assisted and corroborated the findings of the autopsy surgeon. When DA Edwards asked Dr. Hettesheimer, "What in your belief was the cause of death?" Dr. Hettesheimer replied, "Death was caused by the hemorrhages from bullets piercing both lunges, the aorta, kidneys, left groin, thigh, stomach, and right arm." On cross-examination, Weeks asked the doctor, "How long could a man live after he had been shot as you described?" Dr. Hettesheimer stated, "It would only be a matter of seconds."[251] Mrs. Hirsch, who was dressed in a traditional

The two .38 automatic Colt pistols shown with seven magazines used by Crowley to murder Patrolman Fred S. Hirsch Jr. *Courtesy of the* New York Daily News.

black mourning dress and seated in the front row of the courtroom during the entire trial, closed her eyes while Dr. Schiltze testified how the fourteen bullets had pierced her husband's body.[252] DA Edwards then called witness Colonel Lloyd D. Jones, a commercial firearms expert with the Smith & Wesson gun manufacturing company in Massachusetts. Jones testified he had examined Hirsch's gun many times since the shooting, and it never misfired.[253] He would not swear that it never could, but he stated that he had never known a pistol to misfire twice in succession unless it was completely out of commission.[254]

Inspector King was called next, as his testimony lay the groundwork for Crowley's written confession to be admitted into evidence, as stipulated to by the defense. The other confession was an oral statement, questions and answers when Crowley was in Bellevue Hospital the night he was captured. The two-and-a-half-page typewritten confession, taken when he was in the Mineola Hospital, was the more detailed one. The boastful gangster admitted to shooting Patrolman Hirsch, plus a number of his other past violent crimes, and knowledge of the murder of Virginia Brannen. He also admitted he had planned on sticking up the Freeport movie theater, where his friend Tink Davis worked as an usher. At the end of his statement, he added, "They say I was greater than Gerald Chapman!"[255] This was a boisterous reference to the criminal known as "The Count of Gramercy

Park" and "The Gentleman Bandit," an Irish New York gangster who committed bank robberies and was involved in bootlegging. Chapman was infamous for the 1921 $2.5 million U.S. mail truck robbery in New York City and his many daring prison escapes. Though Chapman had been sentenced to twenty-five years in federal prison, President Calvin Coolidge reduced his sentence and he was released. In 1926, while on yet another wild crime spree in Connecticut, Chapman shot and killed New Britain patrolman James Skelly. Chapman was executed by hanging in Wethersfield, Connecticut, for the killing.[256]

Crowley stated in part that when he and Helen Walsh were first approached by the cops on Morris Avenue,

> *One of them recognized me and said they were going to take us in. I pleaded with them not to take Helen, but they said they were going to. Hirsch put his gun into my stomach and said come on. I then tried to grab my guns out of my pockets, and I heard Hirsch's trigger click twice but his gun failed to go off. This gave me more confidence and I let Hirsch have both guns. My first shot hit him in the right arm, and he dropped his gun on to the front seat alongside of me.[257]*

NYPD ballistics expert Captain Harry Butts identified the bullets taken from Patrolman Hirsch's body as being fired from Crowley's two guns. He further stated that he compared test bullets from the same guns, and they matched beyond doubt. Captain Butts ended his testimony when he stated that none of the bullets that struck Hirsch was fired from his own service gun.[258] Weeks had no questions for this witness. DA Edwards then called Nassau lieutenant Harry G. Wright, the police department's firearms instructor, who sprang a surprise on the defense when he testified that at 10:20 p.m., just two hours before Hirsch was fatally shot, he met Hirsch on the pistol range at police headquarters, borrowed Hirsch's gun and fired two shots from it, getting a bullseye each time.[259] Weeks jumped up from his seat at the counselors' table and boldly objected to this testimony, but he was quickly overruled. He then turned to face Lieutenant Wright and asked sarcastically, "You didn't by any chance have Yodice there to give him pistol practice, did you?" Wright replied, "No."[260]

Also called was Clinton Davis, who testified that Crowley had told him that he knew that the cops were hunting him.[261] But more damning was John McCahill's testimony that Crowley had said that "he expected to shoot it out with the cops sooner or later. Either I'll shoot them, or they'll shoot me, it's my life or theirs."[262] However, the most damaging testimony against the gangster—other than his own confessions—came from the testimony of his girlfriend Helen Walsh. Helen was accompanied by police matron Schwab. She wore a blue silk dress, a long skipper blue jacket trimmed with an over-the-shoulder gray fur collar and a natty blue straw poke bonnet, black shoes and sheer chiffon hose, with a coral necklace around her throat. She showed no sign of nervousness as she took her seat in the witness chair and exchanged a quick but curt nod with her old boyfriend.

Throughout her short but devastating testimony, she didn't even look at Crowley, while he couldn't look anywhere else.[263] The feather-voiced Helen told the court of her prior history with Crowley, how they met, how he had asked her to marry him and how she returned his engagement ring because he wouldn't stop hanging out with his gangster friends in the Bronx. She also told the court what happen on Black Shirt Lane that Tuesday night. Two cops drove up to Shorty's car with their headlights gleaming into their car, illuminating the interior like it was daylight, and then they walked up to the car and started asking questions. She said the nice cop (Hirsch) asked her name and that she lied and said it was Mary McCahill because she was scared. Helen knew Shorty was wanted by the cops for shooting the patrolman in the city. While she was talking with Hirsch, the other cop (Yodice), the rough one, was talking with Shorty. She said Hirsch asked her how old she was, and she lied and said she was seventeen. He then asked her if her mother knew she was out so late; Helen said she did. Then Helen said both cops started to walk away. But then Hirsch hesitated for a second by the open car door and said something to Yodice. He turned back and asked Shorty for his driver's license while the other cop continued to walk up toward the front of the car. The next thing she knew, Shorty had a gun in each hand and was blazing away at the cop. Helen also made it clear that Patrolman Hirsch didn't have his gun in his hand—nor did he have a gun to Crowley's stomach. She said she didn't see Hirsch's gun until after Shorty shot him and he slumped dead, half on to the running board of the car and half on the ground. That's when Shorty reached across the front seat and pushed the cop the rest of the way out of the car, but not before he took the cop's gun out of his holster. Helen confirmed that when Shorty started shooting, the cop started to yell to his partner, "Yo, Yo, Yo," just before he fell.[264]

While Helen was testifying, a loud screech of rage was heard in the corridor outside the courtroom. It came from Billie Dunne, who became hysterical when she heard her rival was putting the finger on Crowley. "Let me in! Let me in!" she screamed. "I'll fix that lying bitch." When the police tried calming her, she just said, "Would you be quiet if someone was saying things about the person you love? Helen Walsh doesn't love him, but I do, I'll fix her." Billie was later admitted into the courtroom, where she would be heard making wisecracks about the proceedings.[265] Helen continued her testimony, but under cross-examination by Weeks, she removed a few barbs from her direct testimony when she said she had liked Crowley a lot when they first met, and even had planned to marry him, but she had changed a little since she had met him. Helen admitted to Weeks that she was scared on Black Shirt Lane and also at the 90th Street apartment. She stated that during the battle with the cops, she and Duringer had hid behind the closet while Shorty stood in the middle of the floor and fought off the cops. Weeks concluded his benign cross-examination of Helen and announced to the court that he had no further questions for the witness. With no redirect from the prosecution, Justice Smith dismissed Helen, and she exited the courtroom. DA Edwards then announced to the court that the prosecution had rested its case. Judge Smith adjourned the trial until the next morning.[266]

At 10:00 a.m. on Friday, May 29, the fifth and final day of Crowley's murder trial, defense attorney Weeks called only three defense witnesses, besides the defendant himself.[267] Not ten minutes into the morning's testimony, Judge Smith had to halt any further testimony until the roar of the U.S. Army planes from nearby Mitchel Field could be diverted around the courthouse to allow testifying witnesses to be heard. After a quick phone call by the court, testimony resumed, as the aircraft was diverted.[268] The first witness to be called was Crowley's longtime foster mother, Anna Crowley. When the gray-haired, portly, gum-chewing older woman took the witness stand, she told a bleak story of Crowley's birth and upbringing, his truancy troubles in school and the many times he was removed from her care by the Catholic Charities, only to be returned worse than when he left. Anna spoke to the court in her thick and sometimes unintelligible Irish brogue of Crowley's run-ins with the law and how he would complain to her that each time he was grabbed by the police, they beat him, sometimes severely. Anna also told the court that Crowley had two prior skull injuries: once, when he was a child, he fell while playing; the second occurred when he was fleeing from the police and fell from a rooftop.[269] The defense then called Dr. Richard M. Hoffman of 71 East 80th Street a prominent alienist (psychiatrist) from New York City. Dr. Hoffman testified that after he had examined Crowley, he determined that Crowley should be placed in the class of moral imbecile. Dr. Hoffman declared Crowley was legally sane but a menace to society, and his mentality was such that he was incapable of a premediated act in the slaying of Patrolman Hirsch.[270] Dr. Hoffman was an impressive and very expensive witness, and the jury listened intently.[271] The defense then called Dr. J.H. Leavitt, the alienist who had examined Crowley four years earlier when he appeared in the children's court in Manhattan. Dr. Leavitt testified that Crowley had the mentality of a ten-year-old child.[272]

14

The Verdicts

The prosecution then asked the court for permission to call one additional witness. Judge Smith granted the request, and DA Edwards called Dr. Albert Matthews, superintendent of the Kings Park State Hospital, in an effort to refute any mental defect the defense attempted to establish for Two Gun Crowley as an insanity defense. Under direct examination, Dr. Matthews said he would place Crowley in the "borderline class," rather than as a moral imbecile as Dr. Hoffman had suggested. With an intelligence quotient of seventy-six, Crowley is next to normal, Dr. Matthews asserted. He went on to say that the standards of mentality in New York State are categorized as idiot, imbecile, moron, borderline and normal.[273]

The defense then called its last witness, Two Gun Crowley. Crowley took the stand with his hair pomaded in fashion, sneering as he scanned the small crowded courtroom from the witness chair, like he was a big-time movie star.[274] Weeks got right down to the tale he hoped would save Crowley from the hot seat, of which Crowley had said, "It ain't a bad place to die, it takes men to die there."[275] In his high-pitched tone, Crowley testified that he started his life of bad boy activities by playing hooky from school, breaking windows and going to children's court for doing things like that and then from being sent from one reform school to another. He said he couldn't read or write, and in school, he was placed into the "printing class," not the regular lesson classes. He testified how he liked to steal cars because he liked to drive.

Weeks asked him, "You carried more than two guns sometimes didn't you, Francis?"

"Yes, sometimes three, just for the hell of it," he responded with another smirk.

"You ever been in trouble with the police?"

"Yes, they wanted me to act as a stool. They knew I used to know what was going on, they'd pick me up and tried to scare the hell out of me."

"Did you ever act as a stool pigeon for them?"

"Noo sir-r-r."

"Did they ever beat you?"

"Yeah. Four times, pretty badly."

"Do you drink?"

"No, I never drink"

"Smoke?"

"No sir I never smoked."

Crowley denied any part in the American Legion shooting the past February when asked by his attorney, a charge from which he was fleeing when Patrolman Hirsch and Yodice tried to snatch him from the arms of Helen Walsh on Black Shirt Lane.[276] Weeks then drew his attention to the Wednesday night when he and Helen Walsh were parked on Black Shirt Lane in North Merrick and asked him to tell the court in his own words what had happened. Crowley told the court that he and Helen were just sitting in the car talking when two cops came up to them out of nowhere. One of the cops recognized him and said they were taking him in. The cop told him to take his hat off.

"Which cop was that?" Mr. Weeks asked.

"The one that didn't get shot," Crowley answered. (That brought a titter in the courtroom, and Crowley smiled.)

"You mean Yodice?"

"Yes, that's his name....Then I felt Hirsch's gun in my stomach, and I said 'if you'll leave the goil go, I'll go with you. She ain't in on nothing, and I don't want her to get mixed up. If you don't let her go, then there'll be trouble.' I was pretty scared and nervoused up, and I heard the cop's gun click twice, but not go off. I shot three times, winged him in the arms, and he started to slip, but his hand with the gun was still inside the car, and I fired about five times more."

Weeks then asked, "Did Helen Walsh help you or aid you in the shooting of Hirsch?"

"No sir she did not."

"Did you have anything to do with the killing of Virginia Brannen?"

"No, sir," Crowley replied.

Weeks then turned to DA Edwards and said, "Your witness," as he walked back to the counsel table.[277]

In his cross-examination, DA Edwards wasted no time with pleasantries and asked, "Did you shoot detective Schaedel?"

"Yes sir, I did."

"You did shoot at the officers in the Bronx?"

"Yes sir, I did."

"You did shoot Officer Hirsch?"

"Yes sir, I did."

"You did shoot at Officer Yodice?"

"Yes sir, I did."

"You did shoot back at the police in the Manhattan street battle?"

"Yes sir, I did."[278]

But every time DA Edwards asked a question concerning any of Crowley's accomplices, Crowley responded, "I ain't mentioning any names." DA Edwards asked him to name his aid in the subway holdup. He again replied, "I'm not mentioning any names."

"Who tipped you off about that payroll?"

"I ain't mentioning any names."

The same reply came to questions about three drugstore robberies and a crap game holdup.[279] Then DA Edwards asked, "Are you still friendly with Duringer?"

"Yes sir, I am."

"Did he tip you off to those jobs?"

"No sir."

"Did you give Duringer the .38-caliber gun used in the Brannen killing?"

"Yes sir, I did."

DA Edwards then asked, "What was the largest amount you ever got from one stickup?"

"About $1,100"

"What did you do with the money?"

"I left it in the apartment, in a drawer."

"How much was there when you were arrested?"

"About eight hundred."[280]

Crowley's most frequent answer to DA Edward's questions was "I don't remember."

When asked if he had intended to shoot Patrolman Yodice that night as well, he stated, "I don't remember."[281] This also brought a titter of laughter from the crowded courtroom and a sound rebuke from the bench: "If that occurs again, I'll clear the courtroom. How anyone can sit in on a first-degree murder case, where a man is on trial for his life, and see anything funny in it is beyond my comprehension. I will not tolerate laughing in this court."[282] A courtroom demonstration of Crowley's encounter with Patrolman Hirsch was given by DA Edwards and Martin W. Littleton Jr., one of the DA's assistants. Holding an empty revolver against Littleton's side, DA Edwards questioned Crowley: "This is the way Hirsch attempted to shoot him?" "That's about it," Crowley answered with a smirk. That concluded DA Edwards's questioning. The defense indicated it had no further questions for the witness and rested the case.[283] With a quick glance at his watch, Judge Smith asked the attorneys about how long they thought they might need for summations. DA Edwards stated, "About an hour." Weeks replied, "About the same." Judge Smith then adjourned until after lunch.[284]

At about 2:15 p.m. on day five, the trial resumed with Weeks taking the lead as he paced from one end of the segregated jury box to the other, stiff-necked and head held high, like a vigilant soldier on patrol. He delivered his summation to a jury of twelve attentive businessmen who had been rooted to their uncomfortable and irritating wooden armchairs in the sweltering heat for almost five consecutive days. First, he thanked them for their community-minded contribution and their sense of fair understanding. Their heads followed him as he stiff legged it back and forth in front of them while telling them how society was on trial as well.[285]

> *This isn't the first time the sovereign State of New York has had a chance to save this boy. The State of New York had their chance in Children's Court when he was hardly big enough to reason for himself, but the state did nothing to correct his criminal tendencies. Why should the State, which permitted him to become a criminal, now demand his life in exchange for the life of Patrolman Hirsch? Are you going to say that this boy, with the mental age of a ten-year-old, could on that night deliberate whether to shoot or not to shoot?*

Crowley's defense attorney continued with minimizing the state's witnesses that he had premeditation and leave open the assumption that he was a borderline imbecile, and therefore not responsible for killing Patrolman Hirsch. Weeks was attempting to keep him out of the electric chair, which by this point was about all he was capable of doing.[286]

DA Edwards stood from his seat at the counselors' table, walked the few short steps to the front of the jury box and addressed the twelve jurors directly. Thanking them for their time, their civic-minded commitment and their participation in resolving one of any civilized society's most horrendous crimes, the killing of a peacekeeper. DA Edwards branded Crowley as a "cruel, deliberate and cold-blooded killer." He described the young killer as a "cop-hating gangster" and insisted that if the killer were permitted to live, he would always be of the same mind.[287]

Together, both summations took less than an hour and a half. Judge Smith then charged the jury with the elements of a murder in the first-degree and the lesser included charge of murder in the second degree.[288] At 4:52 p.m., the jury was sequestered for deliberations. Thirty-two minutes later, with only one ballot needed, at 5:20 p.m. the jury filed back into Judge Smith's overcrowded courtroom with the verdict. Crowley stood with his attorney as Judge Smith read aloud the jury's verdict, guilty of murder in the first degree, and the jurors were polled. Judge Smith postponed sentencing until the following Monday morning, June 1.[289] Crowley was then directed to answer a few short pedigree questions asked by the court clerk. When he finished with the pedigree questions, Judge Smith stepped off the bench, and Crowley was handcuffed to Deputy Sheriff Frank Davis for his return to the county jail. As they began their slow exit from the small and crowded courtroom, Crowley made a last bid for his freedom. He yanked his shackled right wrist from Deputy Davis, but the deputy quickly snapped his handcuffed wrist backward, spinning Crowley on his heels—his free left hand made a sudden thrust beneath the deputy's coat for his gun. The police guards leaped into action, and a battle started. A litany of Crowley's loud profanity directed at the cops echoed throughout the entire courthouse. He punched viciously at the police with his free hand, while his foster mother and foster sister started screaming from their front row seats. The courtroom was in complete tumult, and spectators tried to flee through the small doorway. Crowley was knocked to the marble floor, and the police aimed kicks and blows to his heads and body. The killer scrambled to his feet, only to be knocked down again by blows from the police and sheriff deputies as they dragged him into the corridor to gain control. After Crowley was finally subdued, the hysteria died down. Anna Crowley seemed resigned to the fate of her wayward foster son, but she did say, "It was those policemen again, it's always that way, they wouldn't let him kiss me goodbye." Crowley was placed in a straitjacket and taken back to the county jail.[290]

```
COUNTY_COURT_NASSAU_COUNTY_ _ _ _ _ -X
The People of the State Of New York

                 vs                       :     DEATH WARRANT

Francis Crowley
- - - - - - - - - - - - - - - - -X

State Of New York    };ss;-
County Of Nassau
                  To The Agent and Warden of the Sing Sing
Prison at Ossining, New York:
   WHEREAS, at a Trial Term of the County Court, held in and
and for the County of Nassau, at the Nassau County Court House,
in the village of Mineola, County of Nassau, State Of New York,
on the 25th day of May, 1931 and on the days following, one
Francis Crowley, was put upon his Trial for the Murder of
Frederick S. Hirsch, in said county of Nassau on the 6th day
of May, 1931, and upon said trial was found guilty of Murder
in the First Degree, for said killing, on the 29th day of May
1931, and on the 1st day of June 1931, was sentenced to be put
to death in the manner provided by law, on some day in the week
beginning the 5 day of July 1931, now:
   IT IS HEREBY ORDERED, that execution on the said sentence
bedone upon said Francis Crowley by you, the said Agent and Ward-
en of Sing Sing State Prison, in the manner provided by law, on
such day in the week beginning on the 5th day of July 1931,
as you shall determine, within the walls of your said prison or
the yard or enclosure thereto adjoining.
   WITNESS my hand at Mineola, County Of Nassau, State Of NewnYork,
aforesaid, this 1st day of June, 1931
```

Lewis J. Smith
County Judge of Nassau County., N.Y.
Presiding.

```
Given under my hand and attested
by the seal of the said court this
1st day of June 1931.
```

Thos A Cheshire
                  Clerk.

Nassau County Court Death Warrant issued by Honorable Lewis J. Smith on June 1, 1931, for the execution of Francis Crowley scheduled to take place during the week of July 5, 1931. *Courtesy Nassau County Court.*

Francis "Two Gun" Crowley handcuffed to Deputy Sheriff Frank Davis as he leaves the Nassau County Jail for his trip up the river to the "Big House." *Library of Congress.*

On Monday, June 1, at 10:00 a.m. Francis "Two Gun" Crowley wore his trademark smirk as he entered the courtroom and gave a quick nod to his attorney; they spoke for a few minutes before Judge Lewis J. Smith took the bench.[291] The defense moved that the verdict be set aside against the weight of the evidence, and Judge Smith denied his motion.[292] The courtroom was again filled to capacity, with many more filling the corridors. Outside the courtroom, Fifteenth Street was a snarled knot of traffic as the curious gathered from all over Nassau County to witness the historic event. Judge Smith directed that those people without a seat in the courtroom leave at once, while the sheriff's deputies cleared the corridors as well.[293] Judge Smith didn't lecture or upbraid Crowley, he merely pronounced the death sentence as prescribed by law. He wasted no time and scratched his judicial signature to the bottom of the death warrant, scheduling Crowley's execution for the week of July 5.[294] Yet all original execution dates were automatically postponed until the court of appeals had reviewed each case.[295] By 11:30 a.m., Crowley was on his way to the Big House with two other prisoners: Mordehle Rashinsky, who was sentenced to two to four years for stealing scrolls from a Long Beach temple, and William C. Hurd, serving a one-year sentence for DWI. Nassau County deputy sheriff Leonard Thorne drove the prisoner car with Crowley and the other two prisoners handcuffed together in the backseat, while Deputy Sheriff Davis and James Matthews sat on small folding seats facing the prisoners. Directly behind the loaded prisoner car was a second car with Inspector

Harold King and Detective Pearsall; a third car with Detectives Culkin and Hutchinson brought up the rear.[296]

The convoy crossed the Long Island Sound on the Port Washington ferry to New Rochelle and then went directly to Sing Sing Prison in Ossining, New York. They arrived shortly after 1:00 p.m. and entered the gates, but only Crowley was escorted to the grimmer confines of the death house.[297] The death house is the prison within a prison, totally isolated from the general population. The only prisoners housed in the death house were the state's condemned.[298] While Crowley underwent inmate processing as a condemned prisoner, he was assigned number 84567, photographed, and his personal property and any money ($2.46) were invoiced to the prison.[299] An updated pedigree was also logged into the prisoner receiving blotter.[300] During the regulation strip search for his bath, and before receiving his inmate attire, a keeper discovered a dagger fashioned out of nickel spoon, held fast against Crowley's ankle by his sock. It seemed Crowley had enough unobserved time in the Nassau County Jail to rub one of his eating utensils into a makeshift dagger, which he planned to use in his next escape attempt.[301] When the discovering keeper asked him, "What were you going to do with this?" Crowley merely replied, "Guess!"[302]

About the time Judge Smith was sealing Crowley's fate in a Nassau County courtroom, Rudolph Duringer sat in a Bronx courtroom nervously twisting a dirty handkerchief between his stubby fingers or drowsing between two deputies as his jury selection finally began after being rescheduled twice.[303] He had been indicted on May 8 for murder in the first degree, with the mandatory sentence of death, if convicted.[304] The trial had been postponed because Bronx DA Charles B. McLaughlin, who would be personally prosecuting Duringer's murder trial, was tied up in another courtroom with the now famous Vivian Gordon murder trial.[305] Supreme Court justice Albert Cohn presided over Duringer's trail, while two court-appointed attorneys, Walter A. Lynch and Carl Pack from the law firm of McManus, Ernst & Ernst of 170 Broadway, tried to keep Fats out of the hot seat, maintaining that Fats was intoxicated when he shot and killed Virginia and thus incapable of a premeditated act.

The courtroom was jam-packed. Six policemen under the command of two uniformed police lieutenants kept the courtroom and crowded corridor in order.[306] Fat's mother and aunt were in attendance but given no heed by the accused. Virginia's father, Joseph Brannen, her friend Gertrude McDonald and family friend and landlady Alice Perro sat opposite Duringer's mother and aunt.[307] The jury selection was a bit quicker than that of his cohort Two

June 1, 1931. Sing Sing inmate receiving blotter page, assigning Crowley inmate number 84567 and recording his pedigree information. *Library of Congress.*

Gun, with twelve jurors selected out of a panel of only seventy-five prospects. By the end of the first day, Monday June 1, with the jury selected and opening arguments completed, the trial was in full swing. The prosecution maintained that Duringer acted with premeditation when he shot Virginia, based on his own confession.[308]

The defense maintained that he was intoxicated, its only strategy being to discredit the prosecution's witnesses and the defendant's own confession.[309] DA McLaughlin called his first witnesses, starting with the Yonkers police. They described how Virginia was found, how they identified her by tracing her back to the Bronx and how she was identified by her friend and co-dancer Gertrude McDonald. Primrose Dance Club owner Joseph Costello and managers James Doyle and Cecile Gray also identified Brannen as an employee of the club and Fats as a frequent patron. Next was the Westchester County medical examiner, Dr. Amos O. Squire, who conducted Virginia's autopsy and testified that Virginia Brannen died from a single gunshot that pierced her body just under her heart.[310] The DA then called the attractive party girl, Mildred Moore, who reiterated her police statement and her grand jury testimony, adding only that when Duringer and Crowley dropped her and her boyfriend Robert LeClair off while they searched for a place to dump Virginia's body, she and Robert did go into the Seminary Pharmacy in Yonkers for a soda. After Fats and Crowley returned from disposing of the body, the four returned to the Bronx. Mildred also testified that she thought Virginia was still alive when Rudy and Crowley drove off, "so they must have dumped her inside the seminary grounds while she was still dying."[311] Robert LeClair involuntarily testified to basically the same events; he needed to be frequently reminded by both the DA and Judge Cohn that he was under oath. LeClair grudgingly testified how he lied to the police about the identity of the car's driver in his original statement, but a priest, Father Joseph McCaffrey, provided the illusory protection LeClair needed as he gave a cautiously worded statement to the police. Both LeClair and Moore testified under cross-examination that they believed that Duringer was so intoxicated that he could not have premeditated the killing and of hearing two gunshots come from the backseat of the car, seeing Duringer holding a gun and Virginia crying, "I've been shot, take me to the hospital." They both had similar responses when asked by Lynch, "On the ride back to the Bronx, what did Duringer say they did with Virginia?" "We were too scared to ask what they did with Joyce, and they never spoke a word to us all the way down."[312]

By late Tuesday afternoon, day two, McLaughlin concluded the direct examination of his witnesses and rested his case. The defense then called its first witness, the defendant himself. After Duringer took the stand and was sworn in, Judge Cohn quickly adjourned until the following morning.[313] By 10:30 a.m. on Wednesday morning, Duringer was seated in the witness chair and dabbing droplets of sweat from his forehead with a soiled handkerchief as he explaining to the jury that he had been coerced by the police to give his original statement. In it, he said that he was angry at Virginia because she said she didn't love him anymore and she was going to marry someone else, and that's why he shot her. But that wasn't the way it happened, he added. He didn't kill Virginia—she shot herself, or sort of. Fats restlessly continued as Virginia's father watched and listened in disbelief as Duringer went on how Virginia goaded him into taking out his gun. She wanted some excitement because she was bored, so he took out his gun and fired a shot into the floorboard of the moving car. He said Virginia seemed excited by that, but she wanted more. He didn't want to shoot in the car anymore, and he told her no. But before he could put the gun back into his pocket, Virginia grabbed his hand with the gun in it, and he didn't have time to remove his finger from the trigger. Duringer continued that Virginia had a hold of his hand and the gun, and she pulled it toward her chest. That's when the gun went off. He maintained that it was all a tragic accident, that he never had any intention of shooting her. He even said that it was Virginia's idea to shoot the gun into the floorboard of the car in the first place. Under cross-examination by DA McLaughlin, Fats stuck to his story. It was all Virginia's fault, just a tragic accident. Duringer's defense attorneys then called several character witnesses, including Duringer's mother, who testified that Fats had never been in any trouble with the police and he was a good son. Walter Lynch and Carl Pack rested their case as Judge Cohn recessed until 2:00 p.m. In closing arguments, Lynch and Pack drew a picture of their defendant as a "hardworking truck driver who had been easily misguided and led astray by his alcohol drinking companions. That there was no premeditation to kill Virginia Brannen as the prosecution had maintained." DA McLaughlin bluntly informed the jury that Duringer was a "wanton killer and scoundrel who is reckless of human life." He added that Duringer did not perform a single act to mitigate the crime.[314]

By 5:00 p.m., after closing arguments, Judge Cohn charged the jury, and the jury was sequestered for deliberations. After eight and a half hours, the jury returned to the courtroom with its verdict. Duringer stood stolidly as the verdict of guilty of murder in the first degree was read aloud and the jurors polled. Duringer gave his pedigree to the court in a mechanically hoarse whisper before being led back to his cell.[315] Then, on Monday, June 8, at 10:00 a.m. Duringer stood before Judge Albert Cohn in his Bronx courtroom as he sentenced him to the only sentence allowed by law, death. Duringer's execution was scheduled for the week of July 13. Sing Sing being a short drive from the Bronx, Duringer was in the death house just in time for the noon meal and assigned prisoner inmate number 84670.

15

The Longest Mile

New York's Sing Sing Prison was constructed in 1825 on a 130-acre abandoned silver mine located on the eastern shore of the Hudson River in Westchester County. Originally called Mount Pleasant State Prison, it consisted of a single building block housing eight hundred cells and soon became known as the "Big House."[316] This new prison was to accommodate all the prisoners transferred up the Hudson River from New York City's overcrowded and outdated Newgate Prison. In 1851, it was renamed Sing Sing, taken from the Mohegan Indian name Sin Sink, meaning "stone on stone."[317] By 1891, an electric chair had been installed to facilitate a more humane method of execution, replacing the characteristic problems plaguing the hanging method, such as the uncooperative condemned, drunken executioners and chaotic multiple executions.[318] Sing Sing's condemned inmates were housed away from the general prison population in a separate facility called the death house, which was located closer to the Hudson River. The death house can best be described as being shaped like a baseball diamond, with its entrance and visiting cages located at approximately home plate. Once inside, the death row cells branched off from each side of the entrance, twelve along the first base line and twelve along the third base line, twenty-four in all. An enclosed narrow concrete hallway led from the entrance to the pitcher's mound, where six smaller "Dance Hall" cells were located in yet another smaller diamond configuration. Directly behind the Dance Hall cells was another shorter ("the longest mile") narrow concrete hallway leading to the execution chamber (outfield), shaped in yet another smaller diamond configuration containing four oak church pews, the electric chair, a separate autopsy room and the electrical switch room.[319] In the eighty-five years the electric chair was active at Sing Sing, it executed 614 condemned prisoners, 8 of whom were women.[320]

In June 1931, when Crowley and Duringer made their appearance at the death house, the Sing Sing Prison warden was Lewis E. Lawes, the thirty-eighth warden of the facility in its 106-year history. Warden Lawes was considered by many to be the prominent penologist of the times, not to mention the longest-reigning warden to date.[321] He authored several books, and many were made into films. Many wardens lasted just over a month, which prompted many inmates to say that "the fastest way out of Sing Sing was to

Lewis E. Lawes, the controversial warden of Sing Sing Prison from 1920 to 1941. *Courtesy of the Lewis Lawes Collection at the John Jay College of Criminal Justice.*

become the warden." Lewis E. Lawes was a staunch proponent of prison reform, and he established many forward-thinking policies and disciplines to the facility in his twenty-one-year tenure. He was even an outspoken opponent of the death penalty, creating somewhat of a paradox to his position.[322] One of the more unpleasant duties, but an absolute requirement of the warden's position at Sing Sing, was to be physically present at all executions. In Warden Lawes's tenure, he supervised over three hundred executions but never witnessed one.[323] Warden Lawes did visit the death house frequently, as did his wife, Katherine, to spend time with the condemned, and they became quite taken by Two Gun Crowley, as evidenced by almost a complete chapter in one of Warden Lawes's more popular books.[324]

Crowley's antagonistic behavior wasn't lost in prison. Within his first two weeks in the death house, he was discovered hiding a crudely made weapon fashioned out of a tightly rolled magazine wrapped in thick wire that he had removed from his mattress springs. His fantasy plan of an escape with such an impractical weapon from a maximum holding facility caused no alarm to the keepers, only a puzzled smile from the principal keeper John Sheehy, who knew that Crowley would have to overpower a brawny keeper at the door to his cell and then succeed in overpowering two other keepers stationed at the entrance door of the death house,

Left: Sing Sing Prison admission photo of nineteen-year-old Francis Crowley. *Courtesy of the Lewis Lawes Collection at John Jay College of Criminal Justice.*

Below: Sing Sing prison warden Lewis E. Lawes at his desk on the second floor of the original administration building. *Courtesy of the Lewis E. Lawes Collection at John Jay College of Criminal Justice.*

and he would still be confined within a heavy wire cage. If he made it past them and out of the death house onto the grounds of the prison, he would be faced with the expert marksmanship of the heavily armed guards stationed in the observation towers. They had standing orders to shoot to kill any escaping prisoner. But that didn't deter the little gangster. He tried other measures. Once, he set his mattress on fire; another time, he flooded his cell by stuffing his clothes into the toilet. To break him of his poor behavior, the keepers removed all items from within his cell and his clothing. Only at night would he be allowed a mattress and a blanket.[325] Meanwhile, Crowley's attorney, Charles Weeks had filed an appeal to set aside the execution, but he couldn't wait for the decision from the courts.[326] Condemned prisoners weren't allowed to speak with other condemned prisoners; however, out of earshot of their keepers, they did somehow manage to communicate, but they could never see one another. For the most part, the condemned were in total isolation. Sometime in the fall of 1931, while awaiting a decision on his appeal, Crowley somehow managed to communicate with one prisoner in the general population, Patrick O'Brien, who was serving forty years for an armed drugstore robbery in the Bronx. Because they were both baby-faced, around the same age and of slight build, Crowley and O'Brien concocted a scheme to get O'Brien a new trial. Crowley would admit in court to O'Brien's Bronx drugstore robbery, discrediting the eyewitness who identified O'Brien as the stick-up man. O'Brien's conviction would then be dismissed, and he would be released from prison. In so doing, Crowley would be afforded perhaps his last attempt at an escape.[327]

On October 23, 1931, the New York State Court of Appeals unanimously affirmed the appellate division ruling on Duringer's guilt.[328] With all his appeals exhausted, Duringer was scheduled for execution on Thursday, December 10, 1931, though his mother tried in vain to prevent it. She even drove up to Albany to see if she could meet with Governor Franklin D. Roosevelt. The governor refused to meet with her or to intervene with the court of appeals' decision.[329] So, on Thursday, December 10, 1931, after visiting with his mother, Anna, and his father, Charles, in the early evening hours in the wired cage of the death house, Duringer was walked back to his Dance Hall cell, where he was fed his last meal.[330] Though Fats always had an enormous appetite, and in spite of gaining an additional forty pounds in the death house, he couldn't finish his last meal of roasted chicken, mashed potatoes, cranberry sauce, peas, ice cream, apple pie, rye bread and coffee.[331] He had hoped his execution could have waited until after the coming holidays, any day but December 10, because that was his twenty-sixth birthday.[332] After shaking hands with the other twenty-three condemned prisoners in the death house, at exactly 11:00 p.m., Duringer was escorted from his cell and took a position in the middle of the solemn procession that walked the "longest mile." He was led by principal keeper John J. Sheehy, accompanied by four other keepers, and followed by the Reverend Anthony N. Petersen, the Protestant chaplain, who prayed

Patrick O'Brien flanked by his attorneys leaving the Bronx County Criminal Court. *Courtesy of the* New York Daily News.

aloud as they entered the death chamber.[333] At 11:03 p.m., Duringer's face showed an expression of bewilderment, and he made no effort to speak as he took his seat in the thick oak chair. Four keepers quickly and silently went about strapping the leather restraints around his chest and arms to the wooden electric chair. Then they connected one electrode to his skull cap and one electrode to his right ankle.[334] Duringer was the largest person to be executed to date. With the signal given, the executioner threw the

The Dance Hall, where all condemned prisoners are moved to on the morning of their execution, in preparation for their last meal and the walk to the hot seat. *Courtesy Sing Sing Prison.*

switch. At 11:08 p.m., Dr. Charles C. Sweet placed his stethoscope to Duringer's unresponsive breast, listened for a few seconds, then declared him dead.[335]

On December 3, 1931, Crowley was transported under an extremely heavy guard to the Bronx County Courthouse, where he testified in Patrick O'Brien's robbery retrial that he committed the drugstore robbery and not O'Brien. Fortunately, the jurors saw through the ruse, and O'Brien was convicted a second time.[336] The keepers in the death house also suspected that the little gangster would try to cheat the executioner with yet another escape attempt once he saw the light of day in the Bronx.[337] The security detail maintained tight control, and he was unable to evade his keepers.[338] A few days before heading to the Bronx to test-a-lie for O'Brien, Crowley received the official notification from his lawyer and Warden Lawes that his appeal had been denied. His new execution date was scheduled: Thursday January 21, 1932.[339] By law, only blood relatives were permitted to visit with a condemned prisoner, and as such, Anna Crowley required a court order to visit Two Gun, as did his foster sister and her husband.[340] Helen Walsh also obtained a court order for visitation, but Crowley refused to see her because he had heard she was dating a cop and she only wanted to see him so she could sell her story to the newspapers.[341] Crowley visited with his foster mother, Alice McNally and her husband in the wire cage in the death house from around 5:30 p.m. until 8:30 p.m. on the evening of January 21. He then returned to his cell on the Dance Hall, where he was given some ice cream sent by Warden Lawes.[342]

About eight hours before Crowley was scheduled to be executed, he received a plain brown package containing a rosary enfolded in a handwritten note on which was scrawled, "from your mother."[343] Crowley

A rare view of the "Longest Mile"—only about forty-three feet from the Dance Hall to the death chamber—as it was referred to by the condemned prisoners who walked their last mile. *Courtesy Sing Sing Prison.*

The four church pews reserved for the spectators of the execution inside the death chamber. *Courtesy Sing Sing Prison.*

held tight to the rosary while a keeper took a knife and cut the right leg of his trousers from the ankle up to the bottom of the knee, then shaved a small circle at the top of his head.[344] Earlier in the day, Sing Sing's chief engineer, John J. Shanahan, had performed the necessary testing on the electric chair, which included testing the two electrodes by submerging them in a large crock of plain water, then turning the power on and bringing the voltage up to 2,300 volts and amperage up to approximately 18 amps. He also tested the restraining leather belts for any weakness.[345] At exactly 11:00 p.m. principal keeper John J. Sheehy, assistant principal keeper Thomas J. Keeley, chaplain Reverend John P. McCaffrey and guards Alfred M. Molitor and Lewis J. Keeley escorted Crowley from his cell into the connecting concrete hallway that began the longest mile straight into the death chamber.[346] As Crowley momentarily stood in front of the chair while the keepers prepared his hot seat, he scanned the death chamber looking for a familiar face, stopping at the only one he knew. "Hello Sarg," he said. "Hello Crowley," Sergeant Lines responded.[347] Crowley was then directed to sit down. Taking his seat, he held tightly to the new rosary, given to him by the mother who bore him life, who deserted him at birth and who remained a stranger as he was about to die.[348] A keeper removed the rosary from Crowley's fingers as he bound his arm with the leather straps of the chair. The jailer then locked his feet into the wooden yokes, buckling them tightly in place with the thick leather straps, then fastening the wider chest restraint. Finally, the electrodes were attached, one to the skull cap that rested atop a saline-soaked sponge. Sewn to the front of the skull cap was a thin brown leather veil that fell over Crowley's face. The second electrode was attached to a small harness on his right ankle that also had a saline soaked sponge pressed between the harness and the skin.[349] Crowley was asked by the principal keeper if he had any last words? His only reply was, "Give my love to mother."[350]

Hidden from everyone's view in the death chamber, through a door to Crowley's right, was the switchboard room, where the state's executioner Robert G. Elliott awaited the principal keeper's signal. In the eighty-five-year history of Sing Sing's electric chair usage, there were a total four of executioners. Two committed suicide and one quit. Also, in the switchboard room with executioner was the chief electrical engineer and the official timer, Jacob Vollmer. Dr. Charles C. Sweet, Sing Sing's chief medical physician, Dr. Patrick T. Mc Ilroy and intern Dr. G.K. McCracken stood against the wall in the back of the death chamber. Seated in the four church pews were fourteen witnesses to the execution personally invited by

Above: It had many names: The Chair, Old Sparky or the Hot Seat, to name a few, but this is a photo of the actual electric chair that Francis "Two Gun" Crowley sat in on January 21, 1932. *Courtesy Sing Sing Prison.*

Left: Dr. Charles Clark Sweet was Sing Sing's chief of the medical staff and was present at every execution to make the mandated pronouncement of death and conducted the required autopsy of each executed prisoner from 1926 until 1963. *Courtesy of Jeffery Sweet.*

the warden. There were thirteen journalists and David Dows, the newly elected sheriff of Nassau County.[351]

At 11:04 p.m., principal keeper John J. Sheehy gave the executioner the signal to proceed. The method of execution had been carefully worked out and standardized over the years; the slow whine from the large dynamo generators replaced the tense silence in the death chamber as it built up its power. The initial shock of two thousand volts entered the electrode attached to Crowley's skull for three seconds and exited at the electrode attached to his right ankle. It dropped to five hundred volts for fifty-seven seconds, then built up rapidly again to two thousand volts for three seconds, dropped again to five hundred volts for another fifty-seven seconds and again instantly raised to the initial voltage for the final three seconds.[352] The entire application took only two minutes. As the whine of the dynamos began to settle, Crowley's tethered and listless body sunk limp below a transparent puff of rising blue-gray smoke, and the faint smell of burnt flesh wafted throughout the death chamber. Dr. Charles C. Sweet quickly stepped forward and placed his stethoscope to the chest of the unresponsive body. He carefully listened, and at 11:09, the physician officially declared Francis "Two Gun" Crowley dead.[353] The invited witnesses were ushered out through a door at the rear of the death chamber, and Crowley's body was placed on a gurney and wheeled into the autopsy room next to the switchboard room. Drs. Sweet and McIlroy immediately set to work performing the state's mandatory autopsy, bringing closure for many.[354]

Epilogue

On Friday morning, January 22, 1931, Warden Lewis E. Lawes authorized the release of Francis "Two Gun" Crowley's body to undertakers Lynch & Sullivan of New York. No services were held, and his body was interred in an unmarked grave in the Roman Catholic Calvary Cemetery in Maspeth Queens, afforded by his foster mother Anna Crowley-Kavanagh.[355] Warden Lawes had received in excess of five thousand requests from people wanting to see the gangster executed—believed to be the most ever requested. Crowley was the 313th person put to death at Sing Sing Prison.[356] Crowley's gangster bravado was also alleged to have inspired the 1936 film *Angels with Dirty Faces* starring James Cagney as Two Gun, Rocky Sullivan.[357] In his 1936 book *How to Win Friends and Influence People*—with fifteen million copies sold worldwide—Dale Carnegie addressed the behavior of gangster Two Gun Crowley after he was convicted of killing Patrolman Hirsch, particularly Crowley's self-serving statement, "This is what I get for defending myself!"[358]

Rudolph "Fats" Duringer's was the 309th person execution at Sing Sing Prison, and his body was claimed by his mother and removed from the prison by Thomas M. Barnard, a Pleasantville, New York undertaker. His family held no services, and Rudy was interred in an unmarked grave at the Kensico Cemetery in Valhalla, New York.[359]

NCPD patrolman Ferdinand "Fred" S. Hirsch Jr. shield number 207 was interred at Holy Rood Cemetery in Westbury, New York. He was posthumously awarded the department's Calderon medal for meritorious service, which was presented to his widow, Freda Hirsch.[360]

NCPD patrolman Peter J. Yodice was later transferred to the department's Highway Patrol Bureau and retired on March 31, 1955, to Sarasota, Florida. He died in December 1972.[361]

NCPD detectives Joseph Culkin, shield no. 8, and George Hutchinson, shield no. 193, were both promoted to detective first grade, with a yearly salary increase of $700 each.[362]

NYPD detectives William C. Mara and Dominick Caso were the recipients of the Nassau County Patrolman Benevolent Association reward of $2,500 for being instrumental in the capture of gangster Francis "Two Gun" Crowley. Checks were presented by NCPBA president Patrolman William P. Ryan. The two detectives immediately endorsed the reward checks and handed them over to Freda Hirsch and her four children.[363]

NYPD detective Ferdinand J. "George" Schaedel, shield no. 76, received departmental recognition for his efforts to apprehend Two Gun Crowley. After many operations, Detective Schaedel continued to suffer as the results of Crowley's bullets and never returned to the force.[364]

Freda Hirsch was believed to have only a dime in her house the night her husband was murdered.[365] She quickly spent the $500.00 given to her by the Nassau County PBA, as her husband's funeral cost $501.75.[366] To support her four young children, Freda took a job as a matron with the police department.[367] In December 1931, Freda was awarded half her husband's pension, provided she never remarry. Freda never remarried and later retired. She died in Brandon, Florida, in 1980.[368] Freda is interred at the Holy Rood Cemetery with her beloved husband.[369] Her oldest son, Fred, followed in his father's footsteps and became a patrolman with the NCPD, as did his son Joseph. All three shared the same shield number, 207.[370]

Virginia Cathleen (Joyce) Brannen is interred at the Mount Pleasant Catholic Cemetery in Bangor, Maine, where she shares a headstone with her mother, Margaret.[371]

Anna Crowley-Kavanagh died on July 2, 1947, and is interred in the Calvary Cemetery at Maspeth, New York.[372]

Dorothy "Dora Dietz" K. Coleman and her husband, Walter, moved to Broward County, Florida; Dora is believed to have died in September 1968.[373]

Helen Walsh moved back to Brooklyn and later married a man fourteen years her senior. They moved to Far Rockaway, New York, and had one child, a daughter. Helen died on April 11, 1992, and is interred at Saint Charles Cemetery in Farmingdale, New York.[374]

Above, left: Nassau County police detective Joseph Culkin, shield no. 8, serial no. 193, 1931, assigned to the Homicide Squad. *Courtesy NCPD museum.*

Above, right: Nassau County police detective George Hutchinson, shield no. 2, serial no. 329, 1931, assigned to the sixth squad. *Courtesy NCPD museum.*

Left: Nassau County patrolman William P. Ryan, shield no. 180, serial no. 176. President of the Patrolman's Benevolent Association in 1931. *Courtesy NCPD museum.*

Rudolph and Irene Adler moved shortly after he was shot by Crowley to Miami, Florida. Rudolph recovered from his five gunshot wounds and died in January 1972 at eighty-six years old.[375]

Gertrude McDonald returned to Bangor, Maine, took a job at a local shoe factory and married Charles Jones in 1951. Gertrude died on December 24, 1992, in Florida.[376]

Mildred Moore-Armstrong is believed to have moved to California. Little else is known of her life, but she died in 1994.[377]

Robert LeClair never married and never left the Bronx. He died on May 17, 1962.[378]

Clinton "Tink" Davis was later arrested for grand larceny auto and served two years in Elmira Prison, and in 1934, he moved to California, where he was arrested for armed robbery and sentenced to one year to life in San Quentin Prison. He was paroled after two years, moved back to New York and married Stella Tarasiewicz of the Bronx. In May 1994, Tink died in Florida.[379]

Salvatore "Solly" Russo joined the U.S. Navy and later married Marie Silipo in Freeport. They were believed to have moved to Pennsylvania; however, his last known address was in Camden, New Jersey. Solly died on November 5, 1993.[380]

John L. McCahill never married and never left Nassau County. He died on October 14, 1965.[381]

NCPD chief of detective's inspector Harold R. King was later indicted for providing police protection to a NYC-based Mafia gambling ring operating in Nassau County. King was acquitted after trial but didn't return to the police department. He died on December 10, 1956.[382]

Warden Lewis E. Lawes was later relieved of his command at Sing Sing after the bloodiest escape attempt in the prison's history resulted in the death of keeper John Hartye and Ossining patrolman James Fagan. Lewis E. Lawes died on April 23, 1947, and is interred at Sleepy Hollow Cemetery in Sleepy Hollow, New York.[383]

Dr. Charles Clark Sweet remained the chief medical physician at Sing Sing from 1926 through 1963, where he attended over 370 executions. Dr. Sweet was also affiliated with the Ossining Hospital as a surgeon, where he once performed lifesaving surgery on a young Peter Fonda by removing a bullet from his stomach, inspiring the Beatles 1966 hit song "She Said She Said."

Vera "Billie" Dunne faded into history.

Notes

Chapter 1

1. Lawes, *20,000 Years in Sing Sing*.
2. Ibid.
3. Ibid.
4. National Archives and Records Administration.
5. Ibid.
6. New York City Police Department, 1931.
7. *Brooklyn Daily Eagle*, 1931.
8. National Archives and Records Administration.
9. Ibid.
10. Ibid.
11. Ibid.
12. Ibid
13. Ibid
14. New York City Police Department, 1931.
15. New York State Census, n.d.
16. New York State Correction and Community Supervision, 1931–32.
17. Ibid.
18. U.S. Federal Census, n.d.
19. *Brooklyn Daily Eagle*, 1931.
20. New York Marriage License Indexes.
21. U.S. Federal Census, n.d.
22. New York City Police Department, 1931.

Chapter 2

23. *People of the State of New York v. Francis Crowley*, 1931.
24. *Patrolman Fred S. Hirsch*, 94-1931 [hereafter Hirsch homicide, NCPD].
25. *People v. Francis Crowley*, 1931.
26. Ibid.
27. Ibid.
28. Ibid.
29. Ibid.
30. Ibid.
31. Ibid.
32. New York City Police Department, 1931.
33. New York State Correction and Community Supervision, 1931–32.
34. New York City Police Department, 1931.
35. Ibid.
36. Brooklyn Daily Eagle, 1931.
37. Ibid.
38. Ibid.
39. Sinram, interview.
40. *Democrat and Chronicle*, 1931; *New York Daily News*, 1931.

Chapter 3

41. Cohen, *Making a New Deal*, 1990.
42. *New York Daily News*, 1931.
43. *Brooklyn Daily Eagle*, 1931.
44. *People v. Francis Crowley*, 1931.
45. New York State Correction and Community Supervision, 1931–32.
46. Ibid.
47. New York City Police Department, 1931.
48. New York State Correction and Community Supervision, 1931–32.
49. Crowley, interview.
50. Garraty, *Great Depression*.
51. Mitchell, *Depression Decade*.
52. Library of Congress, 2019.
53. Ibid.
54. Crowley, interview.
55. Ibid.

56. Ibid.
57. *People v. Francis Crowley*, 1931.
58. Sinram, interview.
59. *People v. Francis Crowley*, 1931.
60. Shannon, *Taxi Dancer*.
61. Gressey, *Taxi-Dance Hall*.
62. Ibid.
63. Ibid.

Chapter 4

64. Crowley, interview.
65. *New York Daily News*, 1931.
66. National Archives and Records Administration.
67. *New York Daily News*, 1931.
68. Ibid.
69. New York City Police Department, 1931.
70. Ibid.
71. Ibid.
72. *New York Daily News*, 1931.
73. *Attempted Murder of Detective* [hereafter Schaedel murder file].
74. Crowley, interview.
75. *New York Daily News*, 1931.
76. Crowley, interview.
77. Ibid.

Chapter 5

78. National Archives and Records Administration.
79. Ibid.
80. *Bangor Daily News*, 1931.
81. Ibid.
82. National Archives and Records Administration.
83. *Bangor Daily News*, 1931.
84. Ibid.
85. New York City Police Department, 1931.
86. *Bangor Daily News*, 1931.

87. *New York Daily News*, 1931.
88. Crowley, interview.
89. *New York Daily News*, 1931.
90. Ibid.
91. Ibid.
92. National Archives and Records Administration.
93. Ibid.
94. *New York Daily News*, 1931.
95. *People of the State of New York v. Rudolph Duringer*, 1931.
96. New York City Police Department, 1931.
97. *Murder*, 1931 [hereafter Bronx court reconds].
98. Ibid.
99. Ibid.
100. Ibid.

Chapter 6

101. *Bangor Daily News*, 1931.
102. *People v. Rudolph Duringer*, 1931.
103. Ibid.
104. Ibid.
105. *People v. Rudolph Duringer*, 1931.
106. Ibid.
107. Ibid.
108. Ibid.
109. *New York Daily News*, 1931.
110. Ibid.
111. *People v. Rudolph Duringer*, 1931.
112. Ibid.
113. Ibid.
114. Crowley, interview.

Chapter 7

115. C. Davis, interview.
116. E. Davis, interview.
117. H.C. Davis, interview.

118. C. Davis, interview.
119. E. Davis, interview.
120. C. Davis, interview.
121. Sinram, interview.
122. C. Davis, interview.
123. Singer, interview.
124. National Archives and Records Administration.
125. Ibid.
126. Hirsch homicide, NCPD.
127. National Archives and Records Administration.
128. McCahill, interview.
129. Crowley, interview.
130. Hirsch homicide, NCPD.
131. *New York Herald Tribune*, 1931.
132. Ibid.
133. Ibid.
134. Ibid.
135. *People v. Francis Crowley*, 1931.
136. Ibid.
137. National Archives and Records Administration.
138. *People v. Francis Crowley*, 1931.

Chapter 8

139. Aylward, *Nassau County Police Department*.
140. Smits, *Creation of Nassau County*.
141. Maher, "Story of the NCPD."
142. Ibid.
143. National Archives and Records Administration.
144. *People v. Francis Crowley*, 1931.
145. Fred S. Hirsch Jr., personnel record, 1931.
146. National Archives and Records Administration.
147. Peter J. Yodice, personnel record, 1931.
148. *People v. Francis Crowley*, 1931.
149. Maher, "Story of the NCPD."
150. Ibid.
151. Ibid.
152. *People v. Francis Crowley*, 1931.

153. Maher, "Story of the NCPD."
154. *People v. Francis Crowley*, 1931.
155. Ibid.
156. Peter J. Yodice, personnel record.
157. McCahill, interview.
158. *People v. Francis Crowley*, 1931.
159. Ibid.

Chapter 9

160. Walsh, court testimony.
161. New York State Correction and Community Supervision, 1931–32.
162. Peter J. Yodice, personnel record.
163. Ibid.
164. *People v. Francis Crowley*, 1931.
165. McCahill, interview.
166. *People v. Francis Crowley*, 1931.
167. McCahill, interview.
168. Ibid.
169. Detectives, *Homicide #94-1931*.
170. Ibid.

Chapter 10

171. Ibid.
172. Ibid.
173. Ibid.
174. Ibid.
175. *People v. Francis Crowley*, 1931.
176. Detectives, *Homicide #94-1931*.
177. Ibid.
178. Ibid.
179. Ibid.
180. Ibid.
181. Ibid.
182. Schiltze, autopsy report.
183. *People v. Francis Crowley*, 1931.

184. Sinram, interview, 1931.
185. *People v. Francis Crowley*, 1931.
186. Detectives, *Homicide #94-1931*.
187. Russo, interview.
188. Bronx court records.
189. Detectives, *Homicide #94-1931*.
190. *New York Herald Tribune*, 1931.
191. Crowley, interview.

Chapter 11

192. *New York Herald Tribune*, 1931.
193. *New York Daily News*, 1931.
194. Ibid.
195. Ibid.
196. *People v. Francis Crowley*, 1931.
197. Walsh, court testimony.
198. Ibid.
199. Ibid.
200. Ibid.
201. *People v. Rudolph Duringer*, 1931.
202. Detectives, *Homicide #94-1931*.
203. Ibid.
204. Ibid.
205. Ibid.
206. Ibid.
207. Ibid.
208. NYPD Detective Division #188–Forty-Second Squad 1931 departmental records available at 1 Police Plaza [hereafter Forty-Second Squad records].
209. Ibid.
210. Walsh, court testimony.
211. Detectives, *Homicide #94-1931*.
212. Forty-Second Squad records.
213. *New York Herald Tribune*, 1931.
214. Ibid.

Chapter 12

215. Forty-Second Squad records.
216. Ibid.
217. Ibid.
218. Detectives, *Homicide #94-1931*.
219. Ibid.
220. *New York Herald Tribune*, 1931.
221. Detectives, *Homicide #94-1931*.
222. Ibid.
223. Detectives, *Homicide #94-1931*.
224. *New York Herald Tribune*, 1931.
225. Detectives, *Homicide #94-1931*.
226. *New York Herald Tribune*, 1931.
227. Detectives, *Homicide #94-1931*.
228. Forty-Second Squad records.
229. Ibid.
230. Ibid.
231. *People v. Francis Crowley*, 1931.
232. Ibid.
233. *New York Daily News*, 1931.
234. Ibid.

Chapter 13

235. Detectives, *Homicide #94-1931*.
236. *People v. Francis Crowley*, 1931.
237. Ibid.
238. Ibid.
239. *Brooklyn Times Union*, 1931.
240. *People v. Francis Crowley*, 1931.
241. *New York Daily News*, 1931.
242. *People v. Francis Crowley*, 1931.
243. Brooklyn Times Union, 1931.
244. *People v. Francis Crowley*, 1931.
245. Ibid.
246. *New York Daily News*, 1931.
247. *People v. Francis Crowley*, 1931.

248. Ibid.
249. *People v. Francis Crowley*, 1931.
250. Ibid.
251. Ibid.
252. *New York Daily News*, 1931.
253. *People v. Francis Crowley*, 1931.
254. Ibid
255. Crowley, interview.
256. Jeffers, *Gentleman Gerald*, 1995.
257. Crowley, interview.
258. *People v. Francis Crowley*, 1931.
259. Ibid.
260. Ibid.
261. C. Davis, interview, 1931.
262. McCahill, interview, 1931.
263. *Brooklyn Times Union*, 1931.
264. Walsh, court testimony, 1931.
265. *New York Daily News*, 1931.
266. *People v. Francis Crowley*, 1931.
267. Ibid.
268. Ibid.
269. Ibid.
270. Ibid.
271. *New York Daily News*, 1931.
272. *People v. Francis Crowley*, 1931.

Chapter 14

273. Ibid.
274. *New York Daily News*, 1931.
275. Ibid.
276. *People v. Francis Crowley*, 1931.
277. Ibid.
278. *People v. Francis Crowley*, 1931.
279. Ibid.
280. Ibid.
281. Ibid.
282. *New York Daily News*, 1931.

283. *People v. Francis Crowley*, 1931.

284. Ibid.

285. *Brooklyn Times Union*, 1931.

286. *People v. Francis Crowley*, 1931.

287. Ibid.

288. Ibid.

289. Ibid.

290. *New York Daily News*, 1931.

291. Ibid.

292. *People v. Francis Crowley*, 1931.

293. *New York Daily News*, 1931.

294. *People v. Francis Crowley*, 1931.

295. *New York State Penal Law and Criminal Procedure*.

296. Detectives, *Homicide #94-1931*.

297. *New York Daily News*, 1931.

298. New York State Department of Corrections Records, *Crowley* [hereafter NYSDOC records].

299. Ibid.

300. Ibid.

301. Ibid.

302. *New York Daily News*, 1931.

303. Ibid.

304. *New York State Penal Law and Criminal Procedure*.

305. *People v. Rudolph Duringer*, 1931.

306. Ibid

307. *New York Daily News*, 1931.

308. *People v. Rudolph Duringer*, 1931.

309. Ibid.

310. Ibid.

311. Ibid.

312. Ibid.

313. Ibid.

314. Ibid.

315. Ibid.

Chapter 15

316. Wolpinsky, *Sing Sing*, 2019.

317. Ibid.
318. *Sing Sing Prison*, 1958.
319. Wolpinsky, *Sing Sing*, 2019.
320. NYSDOC records.
321. Lewis E. Lawes Papers.
322. Ibid.
323. Lawes, *20,000 Years in Sing Sing*, 1932.
324. Ibid.
325. New York State Correction and Community Supervision, 84567.
326. *People v. Francis Crowley*, 1931.
327. Crowley, interview.
328. *People v. Rudolph Duringer*, 1931.
329. Ibid.
330. Ibid.
331. *New York Daily News*, 1931.
332. *Sing Sing Prison*, 1958.
333. Ibid.
334. *New York Daily News*, 1931.
335. Ibid.
336. *Re-Trial* 2120-31.
337. Ibid.
338. Ibid.
339. Crowley, interview.
340. Ibid.
341. Ibid.
342. Ibid.
343. *New York Daily News*, 1931.
344. Crowley, interview.
345. Ibid.
346. *New York Daily News*, 1931.
347. Ibid.
348. Hirsch homicide, NCPD.
349. *New York Daily News*, 1931.
350. Ibid.
351. Crowley, interview.
352. Ibid.
353. NYSDOC records.
354. Crowley, interview.

Epilogue

355. Crowley, interview.

356. Lawes, *20,000 Years in Sing Sing*.

357. Crowley, interview.

358. Carnegie, *How to Win Friends*, 1936.

359. National Archives and Records Administration

360. Fred J. Hirsh Jr. personnel records.

361. Peter J. Yodice personnel records.

362. *New York Daily News*, 1931.

363. Ibid.

364. New York City Police Department, 1931.

365. *New York Daily News*, 1931.

366. Fred J. Hirsh Jr. personnel records, 1931.

367. Ibid.

368. National Archives and Records Administration.

369. Ibid.

370. Fred J. Hirsh Jr. personnel records, 1931.

371. National Archives and Records Administration.

372. Ibid.

373. Ibid.

374. Ibid.

375. Ibid.

376. Ibid.

377. Ibid.

378. Ibid.

379. Ibid.

380. Ibid.

381. Ibid.

382. Maher, "Story of the NCPD."

383. Goewey, *Crash Out*.

Bibliography

Books

Aylward, Jerry. *Nassau County Police Department.* Charleston, SC: Arcadia Publishing, 2019.

Carnegie, Dale. *How to Win Friends and Influence People.* New York: Simon & Schuster, 1936.

Cohen, Lizabeth. *Making a New Deal.* NY: Cambridge University Press, 1990.

Garraty, John A. *The Great Depression: An Inquiry into the Causes, Course, and Consequences of the Worldwide Depression of the Nineteen-Thirties, as Seen by Contemporaries and in the Light of History.* New York: Anchor Books, 1986.

Goewey, David. *Crash Out.* New York: Three Rivers Press, 2005.

Gressey, Paul G. *The Taxi-Dance Hall.* NJ: Patterson Smith, 1932.

Jeffers, H. Paul. *Gentleman Gerald.* New York: St. Martins Press, 1995.

Lawes, Warden Lewis E. *20,000 Years in Sing Sing.* New York: New Home Library, 1932.

Mitchell, B. *Depression Decade.* New York: Holt, Reinhart and Winston, 1961.

New York State Penal Law and Criminal Procedure. Albany: New York State, 1931.

Shannon, Robert Terry. 1931. *The Taxi Dancer.* New York: A.L. Burt, 1931.

Sing Sing Prison. Albany: New York State Department of Corrections, 1931.

Sing Sing Prison. Albany: State of New York, 1958.

Smits, Edward J. *The Creation of Nassau County.* Mineola, NY: Nassau County Historical Museum, 1969.

Wolpinsky, Arthur M. *Sing Sing "The Big House."* Ossining: NYSC, 2019.

Case Files, Police Interviews and Reports

Attempted Murder of a Patrolman. 231-15 Squad. Manhattan, March 13, 1931.

Attempted Murder of Detective Ferdinand "George" Schaedel. DD #188-1931 42nd Detective Squad. Bronx, New York, February 22, 1931.

Crowley, Francis, interview by NCPD Detectives Closs and Quinn. 1931. *Defendant* (May).

Davis, Clinton, interview by Nassau County ADA Albert M. DeMeo. 1931. *Witness* (May 6).

Davis, Edith, interview by Nassau County ADA Albert M. DeMeo. 1931. *Witness* (May 6).

Davis, Hugh C., interview by NCPD Inspector Harold King. 1931. *Witness* (May 6).

Detectives. *Homicide #94-1931.* 262s. Mineola, New York: Chief of Detectives, 1931.

Fred S. Hirsch Jr. Personnel Records, Mineola, New York: NCPD, 1931.

McCahill, John, interview by Nassau County ADA Albert M. DeMeo/ NCPD Chief of Detectives Harold King. 1931. *Witness* (May 6).

Patrolman Fred S. Hirsch. Homicide. 94-1931. Nassau County Police Department Records, May 1931.

Peter J. Yodice. Personnel Records, Mineola, New York: NCPD, 1931.

Russo, Salvatore, interview by NCPD Chief of Detectives Harold King, 1931. *Witness* (May 6).

Schiltze, De. Otto H. Autopsy Report. Stenographer's Transcript. Mineola, NCPD Homicide case files, 1931.

Singer, Howard, interview by NCPD Inspector Harold King, 1931. *Witness* (May 6).

Sinram, Thelma, interview by Nassau County ADA Albert M. DeMeo, 1931. *Witness* (May 6).

Walsh, Helen. Court testimony. NCPD Homicide case files, 1931.

Newspapers

Bangor (ME) Daily News, April 30, 1931.

Brooklyn Daily Eagle, 1931.

Brooklyn Times Union, May 1931.

Democrat and Chronicle (Rochester, NY), May 1931.

New York Daily News, 1931.

New York Herald Tribune, May 9, 1931.
Press and Sun-Bulletin (Binghamton, NY), May 8, 1931.
Standard Union (Brooklyn, NY), 1931.

Other Records and Sources

Lewis E. Lawes (Sing Sing Warden) Papers. Lloyd Sealy Library, John Jay College, New York.

Maher, George F. "The Story of the NCPD." *Assocation of Retired Police Officers Newsletter*, 1996.

Murder. 1931. Yonkers PD. Bronx Supreme Court, April 1932.

National Archives and Records Administration. New York State Census. 1880–1940.

———. U.S. Federal Census. 1880–1940.

New York City Police Department (NYPD). Detective Division #188-42nd Squad. Bronx Criminal Court, February, 1931. NYPD Departmental records available at 1 Police Plaza.

New York Extracted Marriage Index. www1.nyc.gov.

New York Marriage License Indexes. www1.nyc.gov.

New York State Correction and Community Supervision. 84567. Nassau County Criminal 1931–1932.

New York State Department of Corrections Records. *Crowley*, 84567. December 1931.

People of the State of New York v. Francis Crowley . Nassau County, 1931.

People of the State of New York v. Rudolph Duringer. Bronx Supreme Court, June 1931.

Re-Trial 2120-31. Bronx Criminal Court Records, Bronx, New York. Bronx County Supreme Court, December 3, 1931.

Rice, Thomas S. LL.B. "New York City Commission on Crime Preventon." Crime report, New York City, 1931.

Index